Beginner's Guide to Flytying

Chris Mann & Terry Griffiths

Frank Amato
PUBLICATIONS, INC.

PORTLAND, OREGON

First Published in Great Britain by Merlin Unwin Books 1999
Published in U.S.A. by Frank Amato Publications 1999
ISBN: 1-57188-184-0

Published by
Frank Amato Publications, Inc.
PO Box 82112
Portland, Oregon 97282
(503) 653-8108
www.amatobooks.com

Contents

INTRODUCTION 1

  A Glossary of Terms 2

  Structure of the Book 4

TOOLS & MATERIALS 5

  The Tools of the Trade 8

  Materials & Materials List 8

BASIC FLYTYING TECHNIQUES 13

  Beginnings & Endings 14

  General Principles 16

  Bodies 17

    Floss bodies 17

    Herl bodies 18

    Quill bodies 18

    Tinsel bodies 18

  Ribbing 19

  Tails 19

  Dubbing 19

  Hackling 20

    The Collar hackle 21

    The Palmered hackle 21

    The Beard hackle 22

    The Throat hackle 22

    The Parachute hackle 23

  Winging 24

    Feather Slip Wings 24

    Hair Wings 26

TWELVE FLY PATTERNS 27

  BLACK PENNELL - A classic hackled wet fly 29

  MONTANA - A modern nymph 33

  BLACK GHOST - A hairwing lure 37

  PHEASANT TAIL - A classic nymph 41

  ELK HAIR CADDIS - A surface effect dry fly 45

  GINGER QUILL - A classic wet fly 49

  GOLDHEAD HARE'S EAR - A fast sinking nymph 53

  GREY WULFF - A classic hairwing dry fly 57

  T.G. PARACHUTE EMERGER - A hatching fly 61

  DUCK'S DUN - A modern thorax style dry fly 65

  SHRIMP or SCUD - A subsurface imitation 69

  WOOLLY BUGGER - A sinking lure 73

Cont.

TRICKS OF THE TRADE

TRICKS of the TRADE 1 - Getting Organised 32

TRICKS of the TRADE 2 - Perfect Positioning 36

TRICKS of the TRADE 3 - Keeping a Sense of Proportion 40

TRICKS of the TRADE 4 - Doing Things in Style 44

TRICKS of the TRADE 5 - Getting in a Twist - The Dubbing Loop 48

TRICKS of the TRADE 6 - Tough Tinsel 52

TRICKS of the TRADE 7 - The Incredible Varnishing Trick 56

TRICKS of the TRADE 8 - Hackling Hints 60

TRICKS of the TRADE 9 - Hair Raising Stuff 64

TRICKS of the TRADE 10 - Storing Materials 68

TRICKS of the TRADE 11 - Color Vision 72

INDEX 76

Introduction

The Beginner's Guide to Flytying is just that - a *beginner's* guide. In order to avoid the pitfall of assuming that you already know something about fly tying, we have gone right to the beginning and made no assumptions about what you may already know. We have started by presuming that you know absolutely nothing. For those of you who have some knowledge already, reading the first sections will do no harm, and you may find some aspects interesting.

In this book we shall lead you through all the procedures necessary for you to tie a vast range of flies successfully. We will start from the very beginning, explaining about tools, hooks and materials, and lead on to sections which cover the basic skills of flytying. These are the building blocks on which all successful fly tying is based. The techniques learned here will stand you in good stead for all your future experimentation. Even the most complex flies are based on these skills.

Tying your own flies is not just a hobby. For the keen fly fisherman who wishes to improve his chances of catching fish, it is a necessity. Many of the most successful new fly patterns are not available from commercial sources and the quality and correctness of the tyings that are available can vary wildly. Tying your own flies, puts you in the driving seat. You can try new variations of standard patterns or develop your own special designs to suit the problems posed by your own local waters. Experimentation is the key, but to do this you need a good grounding in basic tying techniques. This book is intended to answer that need.

A Glossary of Flytying Terms

Abdomen:
The rear part of the fly body behind the thorax of a nymph or imitation of a real fly, is often referred to as the abdomen.

Butt:
A turn or two of fluffy material, normally herl, which is used to divide body sections of a fly or to divide the tail from the body of a fly.

Cape:
A part of the neck of a bird which consists of the feathers (hackles) still attached to the skin. The best way of buying hackles.

Cheeks:
Small feathers tied each side of the main wing of a fly. Some flies have both cheeks and eyes. If so the eyes are the smaller feathers.

Dubbing:
The art of creating a fly body by spreading fibers or hair around the tying thread and then wrapping the thread around the hook shank. Also the material used for this purpose.

Eye:
This can mean the imitation of real eyes or it can mean the use of small feathers tied both sides of the main wing. They are intended to act as attraction target points.

Quill:
A feather normally from the wing of a bird. Also a single stalk of a feather such as a peacock eye which is used to form a segmented fly body.

Ribbing:
A spiral overwrap along a body. Usually of tinsel or wire but other materials such as thread or wool may be used.

Saddle:
The rump of a hen or cockerel. Hackles from this part of the bird are longer than those from the cape. Good for palmered hackles on longshank hooks.

Slip:
A group of married fibers taken from a quill. Normally used for winging but can also be used for forming wing cases.

Tag:
That part of a fly which lies behind and underneath the tail. Some flies have a few turns of tinsel or floss (or both) or a bunch of fibers which are tied in before the tail.

Thorax:
That part of a fly body which lies between the abdomen and head of a fly. Normally applicable to flies or nymphs that attempt to imitate a real insect.

Throat:
The part of a fly which lies under the hook shank just behind the head. Normally refers to a hackle tied in this position

Tinsel:
Originally metallic thread. Modern versions are often plastic, non-tarnishing materials which come in a variety of colors and forms - flat, oval etc. Mainly used for ribbing but flat tinsel may also be used to form fly bodies.

Tippets:
Feather fibers taken from the neck/crest of a pheasant. Used mainly for tails but may also be used as winging materials.

Wing:
The part of a fly which is tied in above the hook shank, sloping backwards over the body. On imitations of natural flies this may represent a real wing, otherwise it simply means materials which are tied in this position.

Wing Buds:
Bunches of fibers (hair, floss or feather) which are used on nymphs and emergers to suggest the wings emerging from the wing case.

Wing Case:
The part of a fly which imitates the wing case of a nymph.

THE ANATOMY OF THE FLY

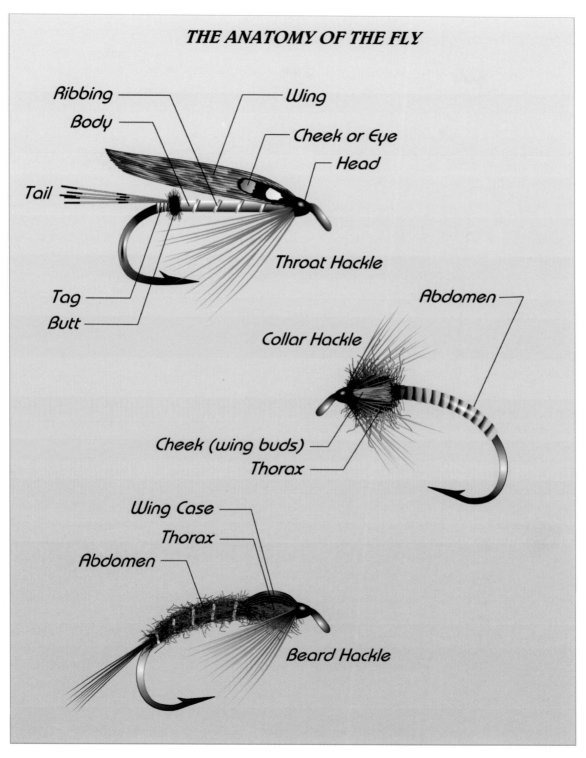

Ribbing

Body

Wing

Cheek or Eye

Head

Tail

Throat Hackle

Tag

Butt

Collar Hackle

Abdomen

Cheek (wing buds)

Thorax

Wing Case

Thorax

Abdomen

Beard Hackle

Structure of the Book

Now a word or two about the structure of the book. We have tried to lay things out in a straightforward and logical manner.

The first chapter concerns itself with the tools that you will need to start fly tying. In common with many other hobbies and sports, there are thousands of gadgets and gimmicks available. Some of these are useful, many are not. We will leave you to make your own collection of such things, and have concentrated on a basic set of tools which are needed to dress flies successfully.

The materials that you will need to obtain in order to tie flies are also covered in this section. Using our recommended materials list you will be able to make several hundred different patterns. The materials suggested have been carefully chosen to offer you the widest range, whilst at the same time offering you the best value for money.

Other, additional materials required for specific flies can always be added at a later date. Naturally we have ensured that a comprehensive list of the materials needed to tie the sample patterns in this book is included (see page 12).

The second chapter covers all the basic skills of fly tying. This includes such things as making and ribbing fly bodies, hackling and winging. Each subject is covered separately in some detail with instructions and accompanying illustrations.

The techniques shown on these pages are absolutely vital for the further development of your fly tying skills. If your basic tying technique is not sound then you will encounter many problems when you attempt more advanced methods later on.

The last part of the book is a series of tying instructions for twelve contrasting flies.

The flies have been selected to show a range of tying techniques. Where two patterns were available, both of which fulfilled the same function, we have chosen the pattern which best illustrated a particular tying feature. Again, we have taken great care with the layout so that the words and pictures are always opposite each other on a double-page spread. You will need both hands to tie a fly - turning pages backwards and forwards doesn't help. Lay the book open at the correct page, and you have a bench tying manual which is in front of you as you are working on the fly.

Throughout the book you will also find pages headed "Tricks of the Trade". These pages are full of useful supplementary information, advice and tips which you will find useful. The information often extends and elaborates on points made in the tying instructions, as well as giving you information about a range of related topics.

Tools & Materials

The Tools of the Trade

In order to tie flies you will need a basic set of tools. The following list comprises the essentials, plus some additional, optional items which make the job easier.

Scissors

The most important part of the kit. Too much care cannot be taken when choosing scissors. Good scissors will have fine, tapered tips, not too long in the blade, and they will be sharp through to the tips. Some scissors nowadays come with serrated blades, these are a distinct bonus when clipping fine strands of fur or feather. It is an advantage for the finger loops to be large, so that they can be picked up and put down easily without having to wrestle them off. Those suitable for fly tying need be no more than 3 - 4 inches long overall. It is strongly recommended that you have a couple of pairs of scissors, one pair for the fine work with silk, fur and feather, and a second pair for heavy duty cutting of tinsels and wire.

Vise

This will be your biggest single investment. The main purpose of a vise is that it will hold the hook firmly. If it doesn't do this it is useless. The most common types of vise use either a screw collet, or a cam lever to grip the hook, both are very efficient, and neither one is preferred to the other. Although the very best vises can be very expensive indeed, the good news is that a perfectly serviceable vise can be had at around £20 sterling (30$ US). The best advice we can offer is that you buy the best you can afford. When you buy your vise, obtain a material spring at the same time. This is a short length of spiral wire, the ends of which can be clipped together forming a ring. Slipped on to the barrel of the vise, it enables, floss, ribbing and other materials to be held back out of the way whilst new materials are being tied in. Very simple and useful if you don't have three hands.

Bobbin (Bobbin Holder)

The spigot bobbin holder is the device which holds the spool of tying thread used for tying. The squeezing of the spool by the arms means that the thread is only dispensed through the tube by the tension during winding. A great advantage is that the weight of the spool plus the bobbin holder is sufficient to maintain tension on the thread when it is left hanging. This means that you don't have to keep securing the thread when you prepare a new material for tying in. There are two types of spigot tube, stainless steel and ceramic, both are good but, the ceramic spigot tends to be slightly more expensive. At the same time as you purchase your bobbin holder, buy a threader, for getting the thread through the tube.

Hackle Pliers

These come in many varied types and sizes. The main thing is that they must efficiently grip the tip of a hackle or other similar delicate material without cutting it. When buying, therefore, check that they have a good sound grip, to the point where the hackle may sometimes break before the pliers relinquish their grip, but no sharp, cutting edges.

Dubbing Needle

The dubbing needle is used more for fine varnishing work than for picking out dubbing. Darning needles will not do for any of this work. A needle for dubbing work, picking out fibers etc. should be short and strong, with a sharp point, whereas, for varnishing the head when finishing a fly, the needle can be longer, with a fine, tapered point. It is useful therefore to have a couple of needles, one for each purpose.

Half-Hitch Tool

The simplest method of finishing a fly, and no less a job at the end of it all. Comprises a barrel with a small 1.5mm diameter (0.06") hole at one end, which is slipped over the eye of the hook and the half-hitch slid onto the head. Many tyers use the end of an empty barrel of an old ball point pen. This makes a perfect half-hitch tool.

Hair Stacker

A two-part tubular device for leveling the tips of fur for winging or tails.

Dubbing Twirler

We find this one of the most efficient ways of applying dubbing, whether it's coarsest Seal's fur or the finest Mole or Muskrat. Also a brilliant tool for making hair hackles, on nymphs or dry flies.

Lighting

By no means the least consideration - you must have adequate light to do the job. An Anglepoise type of lamp with a 60 - 100 watt bulb capacity is ideal. The 'daylight' blue bulbs available from craft or needlework stores are superb for flytying. They are a little expensive at first, but they last a long time, and the quality of light is exceptional. Avoid fluorescent light fittings, they distort colors, and are very tiring on the eyes.

Odds & Ends

Other items or implements which are very useful include:

A scalpel or small craft knife, for cutting into hide etc.

A small piece of Velcro, the barbed bit, for fluffing out dubbings, instead of using the dubbing needle.

Fine-pointed tweezers for that delicate pick-up work: handy but not essential.

Fine-tipped pliers, the type that jewellers might use: very useful for all sorts of work when a firm hold is required, flattening barbs or for putting a bend into a hook-shank etc.

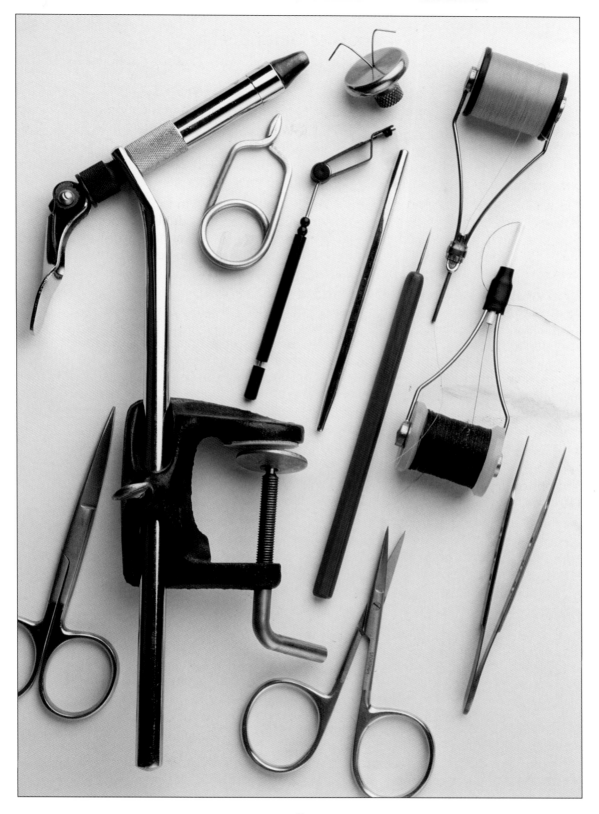

BUYING MATERIALS

There are few other hobbies where a newcomer will find such a warm welcome. As fly tyers we are well served by one of the few businesses in the world where the customer really does come first. Almost every retailer or mail order house is staffed by people who are keen anglers and fly tyers themselves. Confronted with the bewildering array of materials that are available, the best thing you can do is ask. Explain what you want to do and almost invariably you will find that the staff are knowledgeable, helpful and unstinting with their advice.

BASICS

Hooks

All of the flies described in this book are tied on hooks readily available from a range of manufacturers. Most popular brands use a chemical sharpening process so sharpness is normally not in question. If you practice "catch-and-release" some hooks may be available in barbless form. Otherwise crush the barb (carefully) with a pair of small pliers or forceps. Hook sizes can be confusing - a larger number means a smaller size. The size of most standard hooks from different manufacturers are similar, the problems start with special shapes (e.g. curved shank nymph & grub hooks). If you are not sure, refer your supplier to a standard hook - i.e. "about the same body length as a standard size 12 wet fly hook". Long shank hooks are measured by an X number which specifies how much longer the shank is than normal. i.e. Size 10-2X long means a hook which has a gape of a size 10 with the shank length of a normal size 6 (two sizes larger). Long shank nymph hooks are usually 2X long, lure hooks up to 4X long.

Threads

Most threads available today are synthetic materials which come in two basic types, twisted & untwisted. We recommend that you use untwisted thread as this lies flatter and grips better. Threads are graded according to thickness, the finest being 17/0, the thickest 3/0. Most trout flies are tied using either 6/0 or 8/0 thread. Pre-waxed thread is recommended, the wax dressing giving additional grip.

Floss

Most modern floss is a multi-strand, untwisted yarn of synthetic fibers. Several times thicker than the thickest tying thread, it is available in a huge range of colors, including fluorescents. Some patterns call for traditional silk floss - this is a round twisted thread which may be used as it is or untwisted. Floss is used for bodies, tails and cheeks.

Tinsels

There are three types of tinsel used in fly tying: Flat, Oval and Round. These are available in Silver and Gold and a wide range of other colors. Many of the best are now made from synthetics, the main advantage being that they do not tarnish. In addition you will also need some Copper wire, some fine Gold wire and some lead wire for weighting.

HAIR & FUR

Dubbings

The most commonly used natural dubbings are Seal's fur and Hare's fur, others include Mole, Muskrat, Rabbit etc. Synthetics have taken over a large part of the market, and represent a major proportion of dubbings currently in use. There are lots of prepared dubbing mixes available, the most useful of which are those combining natural fur with sparkle material. Some excellent seal's fur substitutes are available which can sometimes be easier to use than the original. Dubbing "Twists" are becoming more and more popular - these are dubbings already mounted on a thread or wire and can be wound on the hook directly, thus producing an "instant" body.

Bucktail

A very commonly used hair for wings and tails. It comes in natural and a wide range of dyed colors. Look for hair that is **fine** and where the natural crinkle is not too exaggerated. The Gray Wulff in this book uses natural bucktail which has dark tips.

Elk Body Hair

A very good hair for wings and tails of dry flies. Available as natural, bleached white and dyed. Natural, with long pale golden tips, is ideal for a whole range of flies. White is used on the Elk Hair Caddis to make it easier to see on the water. Note that the body hair does not flare widely when tied in. Make sure that your supplier knows that you wish to use it for wings & tails, **not** for spinning (hair for spinning "flares" readily with the thread pressure and is not suitable for wings or tails).

Calf Hair

Another natural material often used for wings and tails. Slightly coarser than bucktail it is available in natural (brown, white) and a wide range of dyed colors. Calf hair can vary greatly in quality and in coarseness. Explain to your supplier that you are tying small flies as some calf tails are only suitable for large lures.

Squirrel Tail

Finer than either bucktail or calf, this hair is used widely for wings and tails. The natural tail has fibers which are dark gray to black with white tips. Squirrel tail is available in a range of natural colors as well as dyed colors. Normally dyed squirrel retains the dark barring. Other tails are bleached before dying, thus producing pure colors.

Deer Hair

Deer hair is available from a wide range of species, each having its own characteristics. Most deer hair (but not all) is hollow and thus floats readily. It is therefore mainly used for wings, bodies and tails of dry and emerger flies. Because of its hollow structure, some deer hair flares widely under the pressure of the tying thread. These types of hair are mainly used for "spinning" around the hook shank to form buoyant heads or bodies of surface flies. The variety is so wide, you will need to take advice from your supplier.

FEATHER

Marabou Plumes

These fluffy filoplume feathers originally came from the Marabou stork but are now obtained from Turkeys. Available in a vast range of colors, they are easy to obtain and cheap. Marabou is used for winging, tails and bodies on a vast range of modern flies. Marabou is extremely mobile in the water and is a very effective attractor.

Cul-de-Canard

CDC (Cul-de-Canard) are the naturally oiled filoplume feathers that come from around the preen gland of a duck. Totally waterproofed, CDC floats extremely well. CDC plumes are also well endowed with barbules which trap bubbles of air, thus enhancing the floating qualities. Available in natural brown and also dyed. CDC is used to aid flotation as body herl, wings, tails etc. on a wide range of dry and emerger flies.

Hackles

Hackles for flytying are taken from two parts of the birds anatomy, the neck known as the **Cape**, which produces a wide variety of sizes of feather, and the rump, known as the **Saddle**, which offers longer feathers. The feather fiber from the hen is soft and therefore best suited to sunk flies. The feather from a cock bird on the other hand is altogether stiffer and gives good support to a floating, or dry fly.

The most widely used hackles of are of Indian origin. They are economical, with a wide color range. Indian capes are the smallest but nevertheless carry a good range of sizes. The Indian cock hackle is consistent in its stiffness, and the hen conversely, is nicely soft. Chinese capes, are a little less reliable for hackle quality, but they are still more than adequate. Size of feather on the cape is the main thing to check for as they can be quite large. Chinese capes that are dyed can be of superb quality.

Genetic hackles come from specially-bred birds and offer feathers suitable for tying dry flies down to sizes 18-22. They are expensive but worth the money if you need to tie lots of tiny dries. Genetic hackles are not necessary for any of the patterns in this book.

Feather fiber (Herl)

Apart from hackles, plumage from other parts of a bird are utilized for fly bodies and wings. Among the most widely used are the tail feathers from the common European Pheasant and the eye and sword feathers from the peacock. Other commonly used herls include ostrich.

Wing Quills

Slips of fibers from wing quills are primarily used for winging flies. The most useful to start with are grey duck quills as used for the Ginger Quill. Apart from natural colors, quills are available dyed in a wide range of pure colors.

OTHER MATERIALS

Chenille

This could be described as a furry rope. It is a very convenient means of making a fly body and the simplest of all to apply. Chenille comes in almost every imaginable color, and in many sizes, from ultra fine to "elephant", and in a wide variety of materials, from cotton through to pearlescent & flash strand types, often referred to as "cactus".

Krystalhair (Crystal Hair) - holographic, flash & sparkle materials

The range of materials available in this group is vast, the range of colours and flashy effects even greater. Krystalhair is a widely used synthetic sparkling fiber that is often added to tails and wings to add sparkle to a fly. Available in a wide range of colors, the most useful are Pearl, Olive, Silver & Gold. Use sparingly for maximum effect.

Materials list for the flies in this book

Hooks: Medium weight down-eye dry fly hooks sizes 10 to 16
Standard wet fly hooks sizes 8 to 12
Long shank lure hooks sizes 6 to 10
Curved lightweight grub hooks sizes 10 to 16
Long shank nymph hooks sizes 6 to 12
Curved heavyweight grub hooks sizes 8 to 14
Standard nymph hooks sizes 6 to 12

Tying Thread: Pre waxed: 8/0 & 6/0 in Black, Brown & Medium Olive

Cock hackles: Grizzly, Grizzly dyed olive, Medium Blue Dun, Yellow, Black, Ginger

Wing Quills: Pair of grey duck secondary quills.

Marabou Plumes: Medium olive

CDC Plumes: Natural brown

Chenille: Medium olive, black & yellow

Tinsels: Medium flat & oval in silver, fine oval silver

Wires: Copper, Gold & Lead wire

Tippets: Golden Pheasant tippet feathers

Dubbing: Fine texture muskrat, natural hare's fur, medium olive seal's fur

Herl: Cock Pheasant center tail

Elk Hair: Natural or bleached body hair

Bucktail: Natural brown (dark tipped) and white

Calf Hair: Body hair white

Floss: Black

Brass Beads: 2 or 3mm diam.

Quill: Peacock Eye feather

Varnish (head cement): clear

Sparkle material: Olive Krystalhair, or similar

Basic Flytying Techniques

This chapter of the book explains and illustrates the basic skills of flytying. These basic skills form the building blocks on which all the more advanced techniques are based. Just as building a house successfully depends upon firm foundations, so flytying depends upon these techniques. There are no short cuts which make these steps unnecessary, the basics must be mastered before you can proceed to more advanced techniques.

Tying neat fly bodies is a typical example. If you know how to do it correctly, it is easy. If you don't, it will be nearly impossible. We understand that you are very keen to tie your first fly and to get on to your local water to try it out but please be patient. Learning the basics may seem secondary to completing the first fly, but you must learn to walk before you can run. If you are prepared to invest a little time and patience in the early stages, you will be richly rewarded later. There may be a few people around who are so naturally talented that they can make it up as they go along but the rest of us need to learn and practice to master these skills. It is no accident that these techniques have been developed over hundreds of years. Many thousands of flytyers, including the masters of the craft, have found that they are the best way of doing things.

Flytying, in common with many other crafts, rewards those who make the effort to get things right from the start. It is always much easier to learn things right the first time, rather than to try and correct bad habits later.

There is one further point that is often overlooked - well tied flies fish better! This alone should give you the impetuous that you need to work your way through these first steps. Believe us, it will pay off in the end!

Beginnings & Endings

Starting the Thread

Almost every flytying sequence begins with the sentence: "Run the thread down to a point above the hook barb, in close touching turns". The main reason for doing this is that the hook shank is slippery and the thread provides a non-slip bed on which the further materials can be tied. That explained, the question is, how do you do it?

1. Grip the hook in the vise, securing only the bend of the hook. Pull a little thread from the bobbin holder. Take the loose end in the fingers of your left hand, the bobbin holder in your right hand and holding the thread taut, place it behind the hook shank as shown in Figure 1.

2. Maintaining the tension on the thread, use the bobbin holder end to wind the thread once around the hook shank, ending up at the bottom again.

3. Now take another 2 or 3 turns back towards the hook bend, so that the thread is securely trapped, holding the tension so that the thread does not slip.

4. Now continue to take further turns, back towards the hook bend. If you keep the loose end of the thread held tautly at an angle and place each succeeding turn a little way up the slope, it will slide down as it is tightened, butting up snugly against its neighbor.

Whip Finishing

Whip finishing is the best way of securing the thread when you have finished tying the fly. Basically it involves threading the loose end of the thread back under the last four or five turns of thread taken around the hook shank. What we actually do is to hold the loose end of the thread parallel to the hook shank whilst we take the last four or five turns. The loose end is then pulled tight. The detail in Figure 4 opposite, shows what we want to achieve. This procedure is actually far more difficult to describe than to do.

1. Take a loop of thread and insert your fore and second finger, as shown in Figure 1, holding tension on the loose end of the thread with your left hand.

2. Tuck the part of the thread that runs parallel to the hook shank under the thread that goes round the hook, using your second finger to hold the thread in position.

3. Now take a turn of thread around the shank, using the open part of the loop. Do this by revolving your index finger around the hook shank, keeping the loop under tension. Your second finger should stay in front of the hook shank.

4. As your fingers come up the front of the hook, you must reverse their positions inside the loop so that the second finger again pulls the parallel part of the thread down into the correct position. The most important thing is that the parallel part of the thread must not go around the shank.

5. Repeat this procedure another four times and then finally, holding the open part of the loop tight, draw the loose end slowly through, closing the loop until it snugs tight up against the previous turns. Trim off the waste end of the thread and the fly is finished.

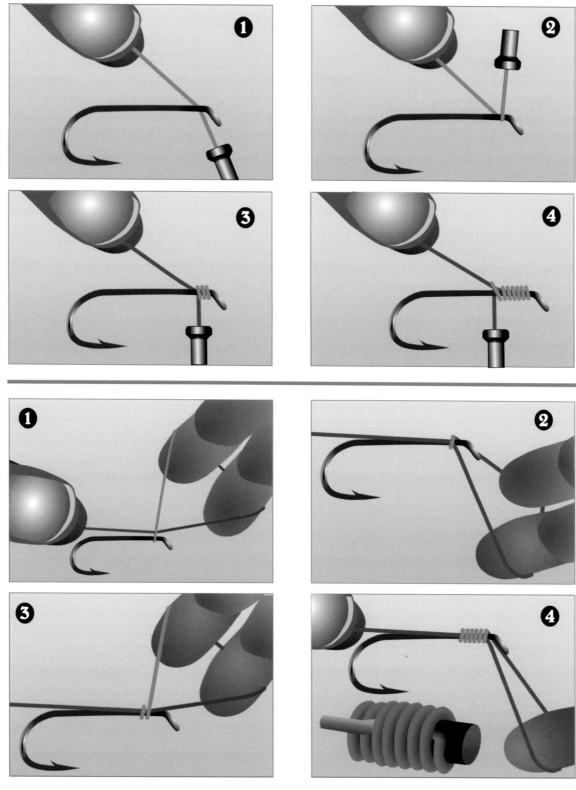

Basic Flytying Techniques

General principles

One of the main causes of the problems faced by beginners to fly tying, is the use of too many turns of tying thread when tying in materials. There is a natural temptation to "make sure" by adding a few more turns than necessary. There is also a tendency to use tying thread which is thicker than that which is recommended. The combination of these two factors will produce flies with unsightly lumps and bumps, and paradoxically, that are less secure than flies tied with only the necessary minimum of materials! Generally, the finer the tying thread, in proportion to the materials, the better will be the "bite" and the more secure the hold. A very useful exercise that we recommend, is to secure a strong hook in the vise and after securing the tying thread, really apply the tension to the thread until it breaks. Doing this will give you a "feel" for how much tension you can apply to a thread. Apart from the loose turns used for positioning and in the pinch & loop method, all securing turns should be as tight as possible, without breaking the thread.

The art of gentle persuasion

The second most common cause of problems is the tendency to try and make the materials (which can sometimes prove to be recalcitrant) take the correct position. Gentle persuasion is the order of the day here - materials should be manoeuvred into position, not forced.

An understanding of the mechanics of securing materials by winding turns of thread over them is important. It should be obvious, that as you wind the thread over the materials and the hook shank, there is a natural tendency for the materials to be dragged with the thread and forced over the shank. The tighter the tension on the thread, the more pronounced this will be. One way to overcome this problem is to try and hold the materials in position against the force of the thread. This may work sometimes, but it is much better to use the "gentle persuasion" principle - throw a **loose** turn of thread over the hook and only apply the tension when the thread is hanging vertically downwards. This will minimize the dragging and only light pressure will be needed to hold the material in position. Work **with** the materials, don't fight **against** them.

If you apply pressure here the materials will be immediately pulled sideways

This is better

Bodies

The first requisite is that the underbody windings of thread need to be smooth and free of lumps and bumps. The main cause of unevenness in the underbody is the cutting off short of other tying materials such as tail fibers and ribbing. These ends should be left as long as the fly body and then bound down with a smooth bed of tying thread. In this way lumps will be avoided. Another common cause of lumps in the body, is the use of too many turns of tying thread at the tail position where as many as four components need to be tied in. Two or three turns is more than sufficient for most materials.

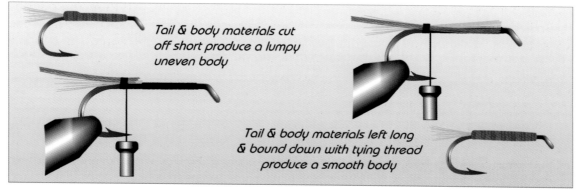

Tail & body materials cut off short produce a lumpy uneven body

Tail & body materials left long & bound down with tying thread produce a smooth body

Floss

The idea with a floss body is that it should look smooth and silky. Handling floss is a delicate business, and any nicks in your fingertips will cause problems. We suggest that you avoid this problem by gripping the loose end in a pair of hackle pliers or put the floss in a bobbin holder, and use it that way. The procedure is quite simple, tie the floss in near the eye at the front of the body, work it back towards the bend, then forwards towards the eye, untwisting as you progress in order that the floss lies flat. Each time you wind the floss around the body, the fibers of the floss rotate through 180 degrees and will become tightly twisted. To taper the body, overlap the turns more where you want it fatter. Don't let go of the floss when winding! Try it and you will quickly see why.

Make sure that the tail and ribbing are covered smoothly with tying thread before you start on the floss

Herl

A small bunch of maybe three or four or more fibers are used to create the body or thorax of a fly. When winding herl bodies, you will sometimes see a recommendation that two or more strands should be twisted together to add strength. We disagree strongly with this approach, twisting the herls reduces them to a lifeless, lumpy rope. The increase in strength will be minimal and is far better achieved by using a fine wire ribbing after the herl is wound. When winding the fibers, ensure that the turns do not overlap.

Quill bodies

This is a body formed out of a single feather stalk, often from the eye feather of the peacock but it may come from other sources. Before winding, the quill should be stripped of its herl. The turns should abut one another and not overlap. Make sure that the quill is not twisted as it is wound. Be gentle when winding - stripped quill can be delicate!

Tinsel bodies

There are many occasions when tinsel is used to form the fly body itself. To achieve a smooth body, it is best to tie the flat tinsel in at the front of the body, winding it back towards the tail, and then forwards again to the start position. The underbody which is formed by the turns of tying thread is of critical importance for the formation of a tinsel body. Any bumps and unevenness in the underbody will be exaggerated and made worse when the tinsel is wound. Keep an even tension when winding.

Smooth bodies are easier to produce with narrow tinsel - wide metallic tinsel which is quite thick and strong is the most difficult to use. With wide tinsel, cut off the end at an angle before tying in - take two turns, fold the sharp end back and secure with another two turns. Try to tie in wide tinsel at a similar angle to the windings, in order to avoid a sharp bend which will produce a lump. When using wide tinsels, overlap the turns by a small amount with the tinsel under strong pressure so that the turns "bed down". Tips about making tinsel bodies more robust can be found under **Tough Tinsel** on page 52.

Ribbing

Ribbing should be as evenly spaced as possible - this sounds easy but is more difficult to achieve than it seems. There is nothing so unsightly as a badly applied and uneven rib. The number of turns that are applied must also be considered. Five is the normal number of turns for a standard wet fly. For a long shank hook more will be better. Try to keep the ribbing tinsel **tight** under an **even** tension when winding.

Tails

There are two ways to ensure that tail fibers sit correctly on top of the shank. You can offer the fibers to the front of the shank, at an angle of about 30 degrees and let the turns of thread draw them onto the top of the hook, or you can use a **loose** turn of thread and tighten the thread with a vertical pull when the thread is at the front.

Dubbing

The usual way of applying a dubbing is to twist it onto the thread. First take a **small amount** of dubbing and tease it out so that the fibers are loosened. Using the thumb and forefinger twist the fibers in one direction along the tying thread to form a loose spindle. This can be helped by also twisting the thread in the same direction. The most common fault is to use too much dubbing - too little is always better than too much. Wind the dubbing forward in even turns without overlapping.

The dubbing loop

The method shown on page 19 is suitable for many dubbing applications but there are occasions when it will not be easy to produce the required effect. This is particularly the case when you wish to use a coarse material that will not readily wind round the thread or when you wish to use extra long fibers to produce a semi-hackle or leggy effect.

In these cases the most efficient method of applying a dubbing, is by means of the loop and Twirler, combined with an application of sticky wax to the tying thread. This process is explained in detail on page 48 **Getting in a Twist - The Dubbing Loop**.

Hackling

There are a number of ways of applying the hackle to your fly, the styles you will need are commonly named as follows: Collar, Palmered, Beard, Throat and Parachute. Tips on hackling can also be found under **Hackling Hints** on page 60.

Heads or tails?

The hackle can be tied in either by its butt, or by its tip, giving very different effects. The butt method is usually used with dry flies whereas the tip method is better for wet patterns. By tying the butt first, the hackle will sit upright, whereas if it is tied by the tip it will "sweep" better. The stalk of the feather has a pronounced taper. If the butt is tied first, subsequent wraps are supported by a thick stalk. Conversely, the tip method has the opposite effect, there is little support from a thinner stalk at the rear of each turn, so the hackle sits back more readily. The fiber lengths also play a role here - if the hackle is tied in butt first, the first turns will have the longest fibers, subsequent turns being shorter. If the tip is tied in first, the opposite is true - the first turns are shorter and subsequent turns produce longer fibers which will sweep back over the previous turns more easily. Palmered hackles are normally tied in butt first, so that the fibers decrease in length towards the rear of the fly. Before tying in, all the fluffy fibers around the base of the stalk should be stripped away.

Wet Fly
Hackle tied-in by tip
and swept backwards
Hackle doubled

Dry Fly
Hackle tied-in by stalk
Hackle sits upright
Hackle not doubled

The collar hackle

In appearance, the collar hackle flares completely around the hook, and is usually swept backwards towards the tail. This effect is aided if the hackle is tied-in by the tip, rather than by the stalk.

To aid the sweep effect, the hackle should be "doubled". Doubling means that the hackle should be folded back on itself into a vee-form, with the best side of the fibers lying on the outside of the vee. During wrapping, all the fibers will thus lie towards the rear of stalk. The doubling may be done before the hackle is tied-in or it may be done during the winding by stroking the fibers backwards between the thumb and forefinger, as the wraps proceed. This procedure requires a little practice.

Fold fibers backwards

The palmered hackle

This is a hackle which runs the length of the body of a fly in spiral turns and has been a popular device ever since a fly was offered to a trout. The hackle is normally tied in at the head of the fly and wrapped rearwards. It is secured by turns of a wire rib brought forward in the opposite spiral, trapping the hackle stalk at every turn. A palmered hackle should not be too closely wrapped, open turns are far better in fishing terms. Dry fly palmers are normally more closely wrapped than sub-surface patterns.

Basic Flytying Techniques

When you wind the ribbing to trap the hackle stalk, take care that you do not trap down the hackle fibers. This is best done by wiggling the ribbing backwards and forwards as you wind, using the dubbing needle to nudge the hackle fibers out of the way if necessary.

The beard hackle

A beard hackle is a bunch of hackle fibers which are tied in under the head of the fly directly behind the eye. Offer the fibers up to the hook and take two positioning turns. If you want to spread these fibers, roll your thumbnail over the turns - the fibers will 'flare'. This can be done with precision, the flaring being controlled to just the desired amount. When the fibers are positioned correctly, hold them in the desired position with thumb and forefinger and finish of with two or three tighter securing turns. Trim waste.

The throat hackle

A throat hackle is initially applied as a full wrap around the hook, and then manipulated and secured so that it ends up sitting only on the underside of the fly. The hackle is first tied in as a collar hackle with one or two turns (not too many because the fibers will be doubled). The fibers that sit above the hook shank are then pulled down with the thumb and forefinger to the underside of the hook and held in position. A couple of turns of tying thread are applied at a slight angle across the roots to hold them in place.

22

The parachute hackle

A parachute hackle is wound round a vertical (or near vertical) "wing" and thus produces a hackle which is substantially parallel to the hook shank, rather than being at right angles to it. Tie in the hackle from the front so that it sits almost vertical. The most important point about winding the hackle is that the turns should proceed in a downwards direction - i.e. the first turn is at the top, all succeeding turns are made below in a spiral fashion. Hold the tips of the wing stump with the thumb and forefinger of your left hand to give support whilst winding.

The more rigid the stump is, the easier it will be to wind the hackle around it. For wing materials that are naturally flexible, the judicious use of a couple of drops of varnish at the base can be of great assistance.

Hackle stalk colored white
to show spiral windings
from top to bottom
Windings greatly
exaggerated for clarity

The final tying off of a parachute hackle can be a problem but the following method makes it simple. Hold the hackle tip towards you, together with the tying thread, and twist them together two or three times as a sort of loose rope. Now make two turns more of this rope around the base of the wing and then release and trim away the hackle tip. The wrapping of a parachute hackle, regardless of how well it is done, will often throw out stray fibers, which don't sit precisely where you want them. If they sit below the base line of the body, just trim them away, it's not a crime.

Winging

Winging is often considered to be the most difficult part of fly tying. There is however no great mystique or trickery, just a couple of basic principles to bear in mind. These two principles can be summarized thus: know your material and use its natural characteristics to help you achieve what you want.

Feather slip wings

When you are working with feather fiber, you have to understand the natural attributes of the material. Each fiber of a quill feather is connected to its neighbor by a series of "hooks and eyes". This arrangement keeps the feather together in flight and will also keep it together during tying - if you let it! If you fold or pull the fibers sideways, the hold will fail and the slip will disintegrate, no matter how tightly you hold the feathers.

INCORRECT

The first steps to ensure a good wing are taken even before we start to tie the feathers in. This begins with taking a matched pair of slips from the same position on opposing wings. It is important that both slips are the same width, if they are not, an even compression is impossible. Secondly, it will help a great deal if you can pull the fibers away from the stalk with your fingers, retaining a bit of quill, rather than cutting them out with scissors.

There is a natural curve to the wing slips
Normally they are tied in like this

But they could be tied in this way round

The better the slips are
matched, the better the wing

Thirdly the length of the slips should match the length of the wings. If you select very long slips and tie them in near their tips, the natural curve of the feather is lost and the number of "hooks and eyes" will be fewer, making it more difficult to keep the slip together.

Pinch & loop

With the pinch & loop method we avoid the fibers rolling and splitting by applying the tension only when the thread is vertical. Because the thread passes between our fingers instead of in front of them, we can also hold the fibers in position across the complete area that is affected by the tying-in process.

STEP 1

First make sure you have a flat bed of thread to mount the wings on to. Carefully match the two slips together dull side to dull side / concave to concave and, gripping them between the thumb and forefinger, offer them up to the hook, positioning them exactly in line with the shank. The wing should extend at least to the bend of the hook.

STEP 2

Once the wing length is established, take a loose turn of thread up over the wing and passing down the other side, **between your fingers**, without any tension on the wing segment. The "pinch" between the thumb and forefingers should be loose enough so as to allow the thread to pass between. A little gentle jockeying may be necessary here.

STEP 3

Now bring the thread up at the front, again **between the two fingers**. When you have done this, tension can then be applied to the thread in an upward direction. Keep your grip firm whilst doing this, but not too tight. With the tension being applied in a vertical direction, the feather fibers will compress tidily, one on top of another.

A quick look will tell you if the wing is set correctly. If it is, make a few turns, but no more than half a dozen, to secure it. Trim off the waste ends of the wing butts as closely as possible and finish the head with neat turns of thread.

Hair wings

The main problem with hair wings is making sure that the hair is tied in securely, and that it stays tied in when fishing. One of the main reasons for hair coming loose, is to attempt to tie in too large a bunch in one go. If you err, err on the side of too little hair.

Most natural hair has a thick, fine underfur between the longer hairs. If you try to tie in a bunch of hair without removing the underfur you will have problems. Step number one, therefore, clean out all the underfur, leaving only the longer guard hairs.

Step number two, stack the hair so that all the tips are even. Full details of this procedure can be found in **Tricks of the Trade 9 - Hair Raising Stuff** on page 64.

Offer up the wing on top of the hookshank. Take a couple of turns to hold the wing in position and check the length. Take another two tight turns to the right of the first turns, leaving a gap between. Now move back between these two wrappings and take one more tight turn between them - the idea is to form a series of crimps in the hair.

Now lift the wing and take one ot two turns around the base of the wing fibers so that they stay together as a bunch. Take a few more turns in front and then trim away the waste hair at an angle just in front of the eye. A drop or two of varnish on the windings will help to keep everything secure. But be careful, don't let it run back into the wing itself.

Twelve Fly Patterns

This chapter gives you the step-by-step tying instructions for twelve flies. Each of these flies have been carefully chosen to illustrate a different aspect of fly tying.

The following flies chosen have been selected for three reasons: firstly they each demonstrate and use one or more of the techniques that you will have seen in the previous section. Secondly they represent a range of fly types - nymphs, lures, wet flies, emergers and dry flies. Thirdly they are very successful fishing flies for a whole range of conditions and circumstances on various water types throughout the year.

As you will note from these patterns, many of the most effective fishing flies are not difficult to tie, indeed there is a very good case for saying that simplicity is one of the most important factors in the development of successful new patterns. Each of these patterns in its own way, homes in on a particular "trigger factor" which can prove irresistible to the trout. This trigger factor varies with the type of pattern - the Duck's Dun for example, has a silhouette which exactly mimics the natural fly and it sits in the water in the correct position (this is most important - even if the fly looks right, it will not attract trout if it sits in the wrong position). The Woolly Bugger also attracts trout, not by being an exact imitation, but rather by mimicking the sinuous swimming movement of certain nymphs in an exaggerated manner.

The Shrimp (Scud) is a close imitation of a natural food item, much loved by trout. The TG Parachute Emerger combines a good imitation of the natural fly with the correct and typical emergent attitude in the water. The Black Ghost lure attracts trout by a combination of color and movement which trigger an aggressive reaction in the trout. The Goldhead Hare's Ear is an impressionistic imitation of a whole range of edible items. The movement of the hare's ear in the water is very attractive to trout.

For each of the patterns we have listed the materials required, together with suggested hook types and sizes. If there is something particularly interesting about the materials used, we have given further information about its most important features. For other flies we have suggested further patterns which share the major characteristics of the detailed pattern. These further patterns are tied in a very similar manner, and are therefore useful additional flies that you may wish to attempt.

A couple of points about the step-by-step instructions. The sequences use techniques which are explained in more detail in the **Techniques** section on page 13. We recommend that you read through the instructions fully before starting to tie a new fly. In this way you can refer back to the detailed instructions, to refresh your memory as to the correct procedures, before you start.

In the illustrations, in order to make the tying steps clearer, certain things are purposely not drawn to scale. This does not concern the flies themselves, which are always drawn in the correct proportions, but may apply to other objects such as hackle pliers etc. These may have been reduced in size for example, in order that they do not obscure the detail that we wish to show.

Finally, we recommend that you do follow the instructions and do not try to cut corners. There is always a temptation to do this when the reasons for a particular procedure are not immediately clear - laying down an even bed of tying thread is a typical case. There is however, always a good reason why a certain step is done - you may find, for example, that without the bed of tying thread, it becomes extremely difficult to get a wing or tail to stay in the correct position.

Black Pennell - *a classic hackled wet fly*

Materials

Hook: Standard wet fly hook size 8 - 16

Thread: Black 6/0

Tail: Golden pheasant tippet fibers

Rib: Fine oval silver tinsel

Body: Black floss

Hackle: Dyed black cock hackle

The Black Pennell was devised in Scotland at about the turn of the 19th Century by Mr. H. C. Cholmondley-Pennell (a real Victorian name if ever there was one, pronounced "Chumley"). If the name of its inventor is a bit high-falutin, the fly itself is as simple as can be. Do not be deceived by this simplicity, this is one of the all-time great flies which can be found in fly boxes in every country in the world where fishing for trout takes place. Its inventor carried a range of these flies, tied in different colors, most of which are no longer in use, although the claret version can still be found in Scotland. The Black Pennell is equally effective for wild brown trout and rainbow trout and, tied in larger sizes, sometimes with the addition of a palmered body hackle, is also a very effective pattern for sea trout and salmon. It is no wonder that it has stood the test of time.

The Black Pennell is a very good imitation of a hatching buzzer (chironomid), a good imitation of many other dark flies and a fair imitation of a beetle, an ant or just about anything else which is dark colored and good to eat (from the trout's point of view).

Although it will take fish throughout the year the Black Pennell is probably at its best early in the season when black midges are hatching.

Like the Montana Nymph, the inventor of the Black Pennell did an invaluable service not only to fly fishermen, but particularly to flytyers. Tying the Black Pennell is simple, the materials are cheap and easy to come by and the details are not critical.

In certain parts of Scotland the Pennell is tied with an extremely short body (as little as two or three turns of floss), using a long soft hen hackle rather than a cock hackle. In this form the the Pennell is a typical "spider" and, fished under the surface, represents the nymphal form of many flies. It is certainly effective. Another variant has a very slim body and a hackle which is reduced to a single turn - it is called appropriately the "Anorexic Pennell". Another interesting variant has a Greenwell hackle instead of black (see left) - this is well worth trying.

Black Pennell - *a classic hackled wet fly*

Step-by-Step Tying Instructions

STEP 1
Set the hook in the vise, taking hold only of the bend of the hook. From a position about 2-3mm (1/8th") from the eye, run the thread back to a point above the barb, in close touching turns.

STEP 2
Now set the Golden Pheasant tippet tails. Use about 4 to 8 fibers depending upon hook size. The length of the tail from the tying in position should be about ¾ of the hook shank length. You may find it easier to "lift" the tail fibers into position by offering them up to the hook shank on your side of the hook and letting the pressure of the tying thread bring them up to the top. Use 2 or 3 turns of thread to secure.

STEP 3
Now the ribbing tinsel can be tied in. Strip off the outer metallic coating for about 3mm (1/8th") to expose the core and catch it in at the bottom of the hook shank in the same position as where the tail is tied in.

STEP 4
Now bring the tying thread forward, back to the position near the eye where you started, tying down the ends of the tail fibers as you go. Tie in a length of the black floss.

STEP 5
Wind the floss backwards towards the bend of the hook in even turns, untwisting it as you do so, so that the individual strands open out. If you do this you will find it easier to produce a flat, evenly-tapered body. If you are using an untwisted multi-strand floss this process is easier, providing that you do not twist it when you are winding it. When you reach the tying-in point of the tail, reverse the direction and wind the floss back to the starting position.

Ideally you are trying to produce an even, cigar shaped body. This process may take some practice before you become proficient. Tie off the floss and cut away the excess.

STEP 6
Now take the tinsel between forefinger and thumb and wind it towards the head in evenly spaced turns trying to keep an even tension on the ribbing as you are winding it. About 5 or 6 turns of the ribbing is about right. Try to arrange it so that the tinsel is tied off at the underside of the hook. Trap the end with 2 or 3 turns of thread and cut away the waste.

STEP 7
Select a black cock hackle with a fiber length approximately 1½ times as long as the hook gape. Remove the "flue" at the base end to expose the bare stalk. You will see that the hackle is not identical on both sides, one side will be shinier than the other (it is often called the "best" side). Tie in the hackle so that the shiny side faces towards the head of the fly. After securing the stem with 3 or 4 turns of thread, cut off the waste end. Grip the hackle tip in the hackle pliers and, without twisting it, wind on 2 or 3 turns, each turn in front of the last. Secure the hackle stalk with 2 or 3 turns of thread, and very carefully, trim away the waste with your scissors.

STEP 8
Finish the fly with several turns of thread, making a small neat head - do not overdo this. Make secure by either whip finishing or with a couple of half- hitches. Complete the head with a drop or two of varnish - do not use too much so that it runs into the hackle.

To tie flies successfully you need to be properly organised. If you are not sitting comfortably, if you cannot see properly, and if you do not have your tools readily to hand, you cannot expect to produce quality work.

The room where you work needs to have a good natural light. Ideally you should place your working table so that light from the window falls from the left. or from the right, rather than from in front or behind.

Your working table should have a mat or underlay on it, preferably white. A piece of stout card is ideal and can be replaced when necessary. You will be amazed how difficult it can be to spot a small hook or brown feather on a normal wooden top. A word of warning here - don't clamp your vise on to the table without some packing so as to avoid scratching the surface. Serious trouble can be expected if you ignore this!

At night (or even during daylight), you will need additional lighting on your working bench. A bench light with an adjustable head and arm is ideal. The light should accept a bulb of 60 to 100 Watts. Normal light bulbs and most fluorescent tubes, distort colors so badly, that it becomes impossible to see what a color really looks like. This can lead to a shock the next morning, when the medium olive dubbing that you thought you had mixed, turns out to be bright green! Most craft shops as well as suppliers of tying materials can supply "daylight" bulbs, these are color corrected to be very close to natural light. They cost a bit more but are well worth it and last quite a long time. Set the lamp, behind and to the left of your vise.

It is not always possible, but if you can so arrange things that the wall or background behind your tying table is of a light, plain color, you will also find this advantageous. If this isn't possible, another large sheet of white card can help.

Fit yourself up with some kind of tidy - a bag mounted on a wire frame is ideal. Into this bag, which can be clamped on the table near to hand, go all the offcuts, waste, feather fluff etc. which you will generate in quantities that you would not believe possible.

Set out your tools in some kind of holder so that they are always to hand. A simple block of polystyrene with some holes in it is sufficient if your budget does not stretch to anything more elaborate. Tools always fall on the floor, especially dubbing needles, so a retaining strip of some kind along the front of the table is very useful.

Make sure that the floor is clear of obstructions around your table and ideally have some kind of rubber mat to cover the general area. Small hooks are almost impossible to find on dark colored carpets and if they are not retrieved can cause serious damage to other household members, both human and animal.

Montana - *a modern nymph*

Materials

Hook: Long shank nymph hook size 6 - 12

Thread: Black 6/0

Weight: Optional - 0,4mm (0.015")
diameter lead wire

Abdomen: Black chenille

Wingcase: Black chenille

Thorax: Yellow chenille

Hackle: Dyed black cock hackle

The Montana nymph was first tied by Lew Oatman of New York as an imitation of an American stonefly nymph. The stonefly is essentially a creature of fast flowing, freestone rivers and judging by the name, Lew Oatman had the rivers of Montana in mind. The fact that it was originally conceived as a river pattern has not stopped the Montana proving to be effective in many other circumstances.

Since its conception the Montana has spread throughout the world and has become one of the classic nymph patterns. In the United Kingdom it is best known as a highly successful nymph pattern on stillwaters and lakes that have never seen a stonefly.

The Montana can be tied in both weighted and unweighted forms and is an ideal fly for the newcomer to flytying. It is simple to tie, it uses materials that are cheap and easy to obtain and is a fly which has proved its effectiveness in a wide range of fishing circumstances. There are few other flies which combine these advantages so happily.

Modern stillwater tyings have tended to replace the yellow color of the thorax with fluorescent yellow and green. Variants with hot and fluorescent orange also exist. There is however no doubt that the use of black and yellow as used in the original is a killing combination, especially for rainbow trout. Some tyings of the original pattern also have a red, rather than black, head.

Variants which are also worth trying:

Replace the yellow thorax with fluorescent chenille - the most commonly used colors are yellow, green and orange.

Replace the black thread for the head with fluorescent red or yellow floss.

Montana - *a modern nymph*

Step-by-Step Tying Instructions

STEP 1

Set the hook in the vise, taking hold only of the bend of the hook. From a position about 2-3mm (1/8th") from the eye, run the thread back to a point above the barb, in close touching turns. If a weighted version of the fly is required, bring the thread back to the front position and tie in a length of 0.4mm (0.015") diameter, round lead wire. Wind the thread back to the rear position, followed by the lead wire in close turns. Tie off with a few turns of thread and remove the waste.

STEP 2

Now catch in three black hackle tips for the tail. They should extend about 2/3rds of the hook length from the tying in point. and should lie on the top of the hook shank. Don't cut off the waste ends at this stage as this will make a step in the body. The waste ends will be tied down when we wind the thread forward. Ideally these hackle tips should be spread out fanwise but if you can't manage this don't worry, it is not vitally important.

STEP 3

Tie in a length of black chenille. To prepare the chenille, strip away the outer coating for about 3mm (1/8th") to expose the core. Tie in using only the core and then bring the thread forward in close turns to a position about 2/3rds of the way along the shank.

STEP 4

Wind the chenille forwards in close turns to the same point as the thread and secure with two turns at the top of the hook shank. Do not cut off the excess material. At the same position tie in the stalk of the black cock hackle.

The hackle fibre length should be a little longer than the gape of the hook and the feather should be prepared by stripping away the flue from the base of the stalk. Full instructions on this procedure are given in **Hackling** on page 20. The hackle is then followed by a length of yellow chenille secured in the same manner as the black chenille.

STEP 5

Bring the tying thread forward to the starting position near the eye and then wind the yellow chenille forward in touching turns. Tie off with two turns of thread and cut away the waste.

STEP 6

Now take the tip of the black hackle in the hackle pliers and wind it forwards in open turns over the yellow chenille. About three turns will be correct. When you reach the front, secure the hackle with another two turns of thread and cut away the waste.

STEP 7

Take hold of the black chenille - remember, the one you didn't trim off before, and lay it across the top of the yellow thorax. This will part and flatten the hackle fibers that are pointing upwards. Stretch the chenille forwards and at the eye position take several turns of thread to fasten it and then cut away the waste.

STEP 8

Build up a small neat head of tying thread, whip finish and apply some varnish to finish off.

The following diagram and notes will help you to establish positions on the hook when starting to tie a fly. In the dressing instructions you will find references to two very important positions as shown on the diagram below:

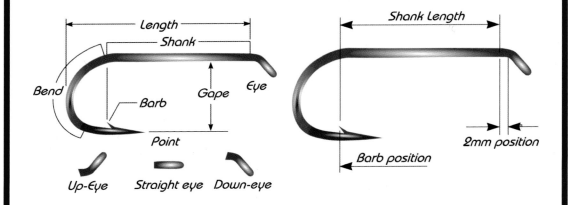

The 2mm Position:

This is a point approximately 2mm (1/8th") behind the eye of the hook. This distance is required to avoid the dressing encroaching on to the eye and to provide room for you to finish off the head. Obscuring the eye is often a problem for the beginner (and is not unknown with tyers of many years experience). The 2mm measurement should not be regarded as fixed - it is rather intended as a guide. The distance will vary depending upon the size of the hook and the amount of material to be tied in.

Note that if you are tying in throat, beard or collar hackles in addition to a wing, you will need to leave more room, otherwise the windings for the wing will overlap those for the hackle and flatten it down.

The Barb Position:

This is a position on the hook shank, vertically above the hook barb. It may coincide with the start of the bend, but not always.

Black Ghost - *a hairwing lure*

Materials

Hook: Long shank lure hook size 6 - 10

Thread: Black 6/0

Tail: Yellow hackle fibers

Rib Flat medium silver tinsel

Body: Black floss

Hackle: Yellow cock hackle fibers

Wing: White bucktail or bleached squirrel

Cheeks: Optional - Jungle cock or substitute

The Black Ghost is just one member of a whole family of lures that were originally developed in the U.S.A. for rainbow trout and steelhead (sea-run rainbow trout). Most of these patterns were originally tied with whole feather hackle wings, but in the modern versions this has been supplanted by hair which is more mobile and does not have the tendency to twist around the fly in the same way as a feather wing.

In the United Kingdom this type of lure became very popular at the beginning of the explosion in stillwater fishing for stocked rainbow trout. Since that time a vast number of derivatives have been produced, but some of the original patterns, like the Black Ghost, retain their popularity and also their effectiveness.

The choice of winging material is to a large extent dependent upon the size of the fly. Squirrel hair is often used for the smaller sizes, but for larger flies bucktail may be a better choice. Bucktail fibers have a natural crinkle and if this is not too exaggerated this is a positive feature.

Among other variants of this type of lure, the Mrs. Palmer, which was devised by the late Richard Walker, one of the pioneers of stillwater trout fishing in the United Kingdom, is still a very effective pattern for colored water.

Jungle cock cheeks are given as optional extras, but there is no doubt that they add considerably to the effectiveness. The problem with Jungle cock is the price - it is very expensive indeed.

Artificial substitutes have long been used, mostly small black feathers with hand painted dots, but these are not totally convincing.

Probably the best substitutes available to date are those which are accurate photographic reproductions of real feathers, printed on to plastic.

Black Ghost - *a hairwing lure*

Step-by-Step Tying Instructions

STEP 1
Set the hook in the vise, taking hold only of the bend of the hook. Run the thread from a position about 3mm (1/8th") behind the eye of the hook back to a point above the barb, in close touching turns.

STEP 2
Now catch in a bunch of the hackle fibers for the tail. They should extend about the same length as the hook gape from the tying in point. and should lie on the top of the hook shank. Don't cut off the waste ends at this stage as this will make a step in the body. The waste ends will be tied down when we wind the thread forward.

STEP 3
The silver ribbing and floss are now tied in at the same point above the barb. When you tie in these materials, take account of the hook length and make sure that you have enough. Wind the tying thread forward to the first tying in position.

STEP 4
Form the floss body, trying to make it as smooth as possible. If you want a slightly heavier body you could bring the tying thread forward after you have tied in the ribbing and tie in the floss at the head end of the fly. You can then wind the body floss back to the tail position and then forward again before securing and cutting away the waste.

STEP 5
Now for the rib. This is wound forwards in even open turns, finishing about 2 to 3 mm (1/8th") away from the hook eye. Depending upon the hook length, five turns is about right. Secure with 2 or 3 turns of thread and cut away the waste.

STEP 6
The beard hackle can now be applied. Take a bunch of the hackle fibers and apply them to the underside of the hook at the tying in position, taking 1 or 2 turns of thread to hold them in position. If necessary, you can use your fingers to distribute the fibers around the hook shank. Check the distribution of the fibers from the rear of the hook as well. For a full explanation of this procedure see **Beard Hackles** on page . You can turn the hook upside down in the vise to do this if you prefer, but if you can learn to work without doing so, it will save an unnecessary move.

STEP 7
The winging material is now prepared by cleaning out the underfur and stacking the tips so that the wing has an even length. Offer up the wing fibers on top of the hookshank so that the wing is as long as the hook. Take a couple of turns to hold the wing in position and check the length. If it is satisfactory make a few more tight turns to secure the wing. Now lift the wing and take one turn around the base of the wing fibers so that they stay together as a bunch, rather than spreading around the hook shank, Take 2 more turns in front and then trim away the waste fibers at an angle just in front of the eye. This procedure is explained in detail in the section **Hair Wings** on page 26.

STEP 8
If you wish to use the optional Jungle Cock cheeks, they can be tied in now on either side of the wing. A neat head can then be formed by wrapping the thread over the wing butts to form a bullet shape. Finally give the head a shiny finish with two coats of varnish.

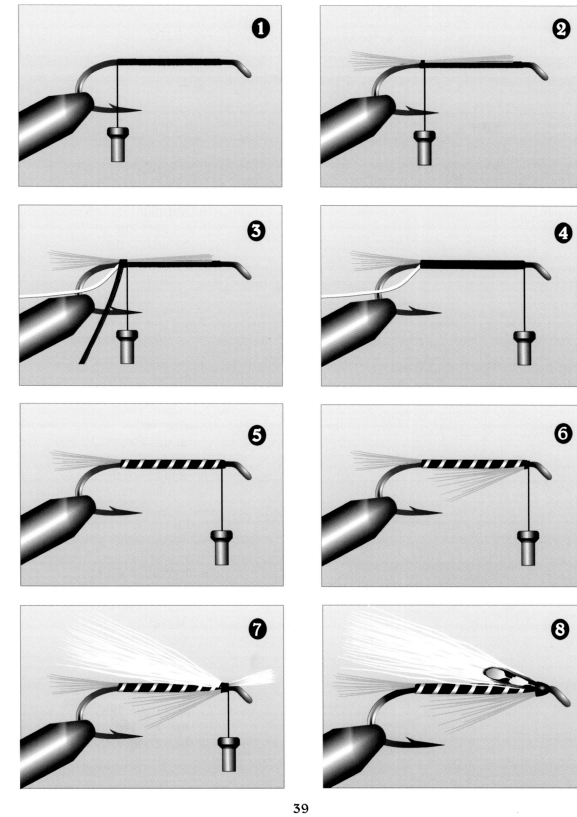

For almost every style of fly, wet, dry or nymph, there is an ideal proportion that is generally accepted as being correct because they catch fish, and also because they look good. The fact that a fly looks attractive to our eyes should not be dismissed as being irrelevant. It is a fact that anglers fish better with flies they like. The generally accepted proportions can be varied according to personal preference - but within limits. The diagrams below are not intended to be hard rules, they do however show you the range of normal variations which you can use as a guide for your own tying.

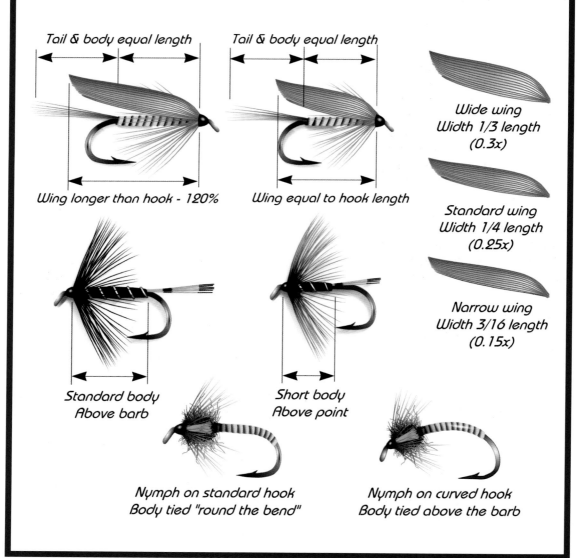

Tail & body equal length

Tail & body equal length

Wide wing
Width 1/3 length
(0.3x)

Wing longer than hook - 120%

Wing equal to hook length

Standard wing
Width 1/4 length
(0.25x)

Narrow wing
Width 3/16 length
(0.15x)

Standard body
Above barb

Short body
Above point

Nymph on standard hook
Body tied "round the bend"

Nymph on curved hook
Body tied above the barb

Pheasant Tail - *a simple nymph*

Materials

Hook: Standard wet fly hook size 10 - 18

Thread: Black 6/0 - 8/0 for smaller sizes

Tail: Pheasant tail fibers

Rib Fine copper wire - dark chestnut

Wingcase: Cock pheasant tail fibers

Body: Cock pheasant tail fibers

Thorax: Cock pheasant tail

The Pheasant Tail nymph is one of the all time classic nymphs for both stillwaters and rivers. Not a specific imitation of any particular species, it serves as a general suggestive imitator of a whole range of food items and is effective in all conditions and at all times of the year. For the beginner to fly fishing it is often difficult to have confidence in such a small, nondescript fly. One even wonders if the trout can see it, let alone be moved to take it. On this score you need have no fear, trout can certainly see it and will take it with confidence. The very fact that it is not flashy means that it does not cause any suspicion in the fish.

With such a widespread and successful pattern it should not surprise you to learn that there are literally thousands of variations on the Pheasant Tail theme. Perhaps the best known of which is Sawyer's Pheasant Tail nymph. In this version the thorax consists solely of wound copper wire with a wingcase over.

The main material for this fly (and for many other similar flies) is fibers from the center tail of a cock pheasant. In Europe this will normally be the common or Ring-necked Pheasant, in the USA it may be from other similar species.

Pheasant tails come in a whole range of natural colors and markings, and dyed materials extend the range even further. The wide variation in the natural colors is clear from the accompanying picture. The color of the nymph can obviously be varied by the selection of the fibers from which it is tied.

The thorax of the Pheasant Tail nymph can be varied - in our example we have used pheasant tail fibers but you can also make the thorax simply out of the copper wire or even apply a light dubbing of seal's fur in various colors.

One important point - you will often see commercial tyings with a bulbous thorax. This is not correct - nymphs are slender creatures and your fly should reflect this.

Pheasant Tail - *a simple nymph*

Step-by-Step Tying Instructions

STEP 1
Set the hook in the vise, taking hold only of the bend of the hook. From a position about 2-3mm (1/8th") from the eye, run the thread back to a point above the barb, in close touching turns.

STEP 2
At this point you should tie in a good length of copper wire. Make sure you have enough - say about 250 to 300mm (9 - 12") long, and tie it in securely.

STEP 3
Now select a bunch of pheasant tail fibers for the tail. The length of these fibers will vary according to the pheasant tail that you have. For the smaller sizes of fly they may be long enough to form the body as well as the tail. For this exercize we shall presume that this is not so, and that the tail will be separate from the body. Tie in the tails so that they extend backwards from the tying-in point by about half the hook length. Secure with a few turns of thread and cut away the waste ends.

STEP 4
Now select another bunch of fibers for the body and tie them in by their tips with two or three turns of thread. Wind the tying thread forward to a position about 2/3rds of the way along the hook shank.

STEP 5
Wind the bunch of body fibers forwards in even, non-overlapping turns to the 2/3rds position, to form a slim tapered body. Tie the fibers off with two turns of thread but do not cut away the ends - we will need them again later on.

STEP 6
Bring the copper wire forwards in even, open turns to the same position. At this stage you can take additional turns of the copper wire over the thorax area to add some weight to the fly if desired. You can now add some more material for the thorax. The thorax can be left simply as turns of wire or you can add some seal's fur dubbing. In our case we shall tie in an additional bunch of pheasant tail fibers.

STEP 7
Wind the tying thread forwards to the eye position and follow this with the pheasant tail fibers. Secure the ends with two or three turns of thread and cut away the excess. It is important that you do not overdo the material for the thorax - at all costs you should avoid a bulbous look. You will see many tyings that look as if they have a football behind the head - this is totally incorrect, no real nymph has such a shape.

STEP 8
Now take hold of the bunch of fibers that were left over from the body - remember, we didn't cut them off earlier. Stretch the fibers forwards over the thorax to form the wingcase. At the eye position, secure them with several tight turns of thread and cut away the excess. Form a small head with some more turns of thread and a whip finish. A drop or two of varnish will complete the fly.

43

With any fly, the look can be altered considerably by varying the lengths and bulk of the materials. The features that have the most visual impact are the length and width of the wing, the length of the tail and the length of the hackle. The pictures below show a wide range of styles for the same fly. As you will see, stylistic differences are acceptable, providing they stay within limits. Changing the hook type can have a major impact upon the appearance. In the figures below you can see that the flies tied on the long shank hooks look much more elegant than the more business-like tyings on the standard hooks. The two flies at the bottom show how things can sometimes go wrong.

Standard dressing on a long shank hook. Elegant & streamlined

Dressed shorter on the same hook not so elegant, but still good

Dressed on a standard hook business-like and in proportion

Dressed with the wing slips mounted curve down. Unusual, but why not?

This has gone totally wrong - wing and tail are far too long

This one has gone the other way. It would suit a hook 2 sizes smaller

Elk Hair Caddis - *a surface effect dry fly*

Materials

Hook: Down-eye lightweight dry fly hook size 10 - 16

Thread: Red brown 6/0

Rib Fine gold wire

Body: Hare's fur, taken from the mask

Hackle: Natural red cock hackle

Wing: Natural or bleached Elk body hair

To understand the reason for the shape of this fly, you have to understand a little of the natural history of the caddis fly. When a caddis fly pupa hatches, the emergent adult swims as fast as it can to reach the bank - and safety. Whilst engaged in this mad dash for survival, it creates a vee-shaped wake rather like a miniature speedboat. The trout, who find caddis very much to their taste, are well aware of this give-away feature and home in on the fly with some of the most spectacular takes which can be experienced.

The Elk Hair Caddis is designed by Al Troth to imitate this fly in two ways - firstly, the hair wing imitates the roof shaped, flat-lying wing of the caddis fly very well. Secondly, the blunt stubs of the wing cause a commotion and wake on the surface when the fly is retrieved which exactly mimics the behavior of the natural.

Caddis flies are at home on both still and running waters and at all stages of their lives provide an important source of food for the trout, especially in the larval form.

A common variation of the Elk Hair Caddis has a fluorescent green or yellow butt which imitates the egg cluster of the female fly as she returns to the water to lay her eggs.

In this case the fly is fished in a more static way. This version of the fly is extremely effective in the late evening.

The Elk hair used for this fly is moderately compressible and thus the first turns of thread should not be made too tightly.

Elk Hair Caddis - *a surface effect dry fly*

Step-by-Step Tying Instructions

STEP 1
Set the hook in the vise and from a position about 3mm (1/8th") behind the eye, run the thread back to a point above the barb, in close touching turns. At this point, tie in a length of fine gold wire for the ribbing (about 10cm - 4" - long is ideal).

STEP 2
Load a small quantity of dubbing by teasing out a small quantity of the hare's fur. Offer this material up to the thread and by twisting with the thumb and forefinger, in one direction only, form a spindle of material. Don't use too much material. As a rule, when you think you have enough dubbing, half it! Instructions on this procedure are given on page 19 **Dubbing**.

STEP 3
Wind the dubbing forwards to the starting position and secure with a couple of turns. Remove any excess material from the thread. At this point you should tie in the cock hackle by its stalk, having prepared it in the usual manner.

STEP 4
Take the tip of the hackle in the hackle pliers and take two turns at the tying-in position. Follow this with a series of even, open turns backwards to the rear position. At this position, leave the hackle hanging with the hackle pliers still attached, and take two turns of the rib over the hackle to trap it down. When it is secure, remove the hackle pliers and trim away the waste.

STEP 5
Now take the end of the ribbing between your finger and thumb and wind it forward, through the hackle in the opposite spiral, trapping down the hackle stalk at each turn. Try not to tie down the hackle fibers.

You will find that the easiest way to avoid this is to wiggle the ribbing backwards and forwards as you wind it. When you reach the front, secure the ribbing with two turns of thread and trim away the excess.

STEP 6
The wing fibers should be prepared by combing out the fluff at the base and then using a hair stacker to ensure that the tips are even. Using the thumb and forefinger, offer up the bunch of fibers to the hook, setting the tips of the wing about level with the hook bend. With the wing in this position take three or four turns of thread around the wing. Note that these first turns are not intended to secure the wing, but rather to position it. The turns should be firm enough to hold the wing in position but do not have to be very tight.

STEP 7
Release the wing and check it for length. If everything is in position take hold of the wing again and make three of four more tight turns of thread in front of the previous turns. Try to keep these turns on top of one another so that they form a neat binding. Keep a firm hold on the wing as you secure it, otherwise you will find that it will tend to rotate around the hook shank. Cut the butts ends of the wing away with a vertical cut directly above the hook eye.

STEP 8
Finally, with your scissors, trim away the butt ends at an angle, following the slope of the eye. Now apply several coats of thinned varnish to the wing butts and the collar of thread - this will secure everything and the stiffened butts will help to cause the wake effect when fishing the fly.

47

Getting in a Twist - The Dubbing Loop

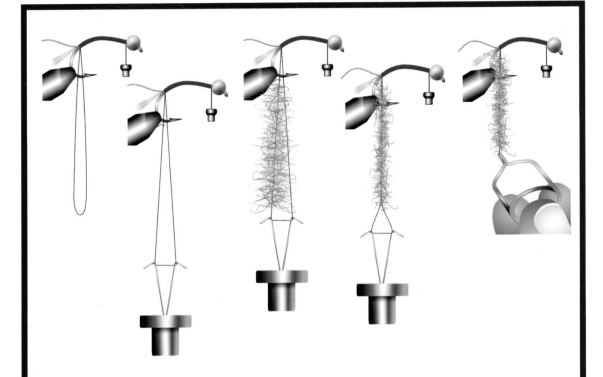

The dubbing loop is ideal when you wish to produce long, straggly dubbing or are using a material that does not easily adhere to the thread. The more off-center the dubbing fibers are set in the loop, the longer will be the fibers in the finished body. This technique can be used to make hair fiber "hackles" - super for small nymphs with a lot of life & "kick" in the water.

Step 1: Make a loop in the tying thread and having secured it, wind the tying thread forwards out of the way.

Step 2: Introduce the twirler into the loop.

Step 3: With a stick of flytyers wax, lightly wax the inside of the loop. Not too much, you don't want lumps of wax.

Step 4: Tease out a pinch of dubbing and spread the material evenly along inside the loop.

Step 5: Give the dubbing twirler a good spin with your thumb and forefinger.

Step 6: Clip your hackle pliers on to the bottom of the loop. When this is done the loop can no longer untwist and you can remove the twirler.

Step 7: Wind the dubbing on to the hook in even turns without overlapping them.

Step 8: When you reach the head, tie off the dubbing loop with two turns of tying thread and cut away the excess.

Ginger Quill - *a classic wet fly*

Materials

Hook: Standard wet-fly hook size 8 - 12

Thread: Brown 6/0

Tail Ginger/Natural light
red cock hackle fibers

Body: Stripped quill from peacock eye

Wing: Slips taken from a matched pair of
grey duck secondary wing quills

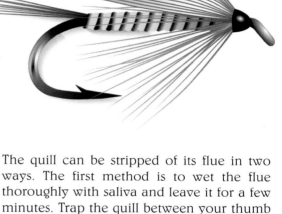

Good preparation work is the essence of consistent quality fly tying. The materials should be prepared as follows.

The body of the Ginger Quill is formed by a quill from a Peacock eye feather which has been stripped of its flue. The quill has a light and a dark stripe along it which gives the beautiful segmented body appearance.

The quill can be stripped of its flue in two ways. The first method is to wet the flue thoroughly with saliva and leave it for a few minutes. Trap the quill between your thumb nail and first finger and draw them along the length. This removes the flue and polishes the quill at the same time. An alternative is to coat the quill with Copydex and after a few minutes, rub it off. The flue will be removed along with the Copydex.

The wings are made of two slips of Grey Duck wing, taken from the same position from two opposing wing quills. Ensure that the two slips are of equal width.

Ginger Quill - *a classic wet fly*

Step-by-Step Tying Instructions

STEP 1

Set the hook in the vise, taking hold only of the bend of the hook. Run the thread from just behind the eye of the hook to a point above the barb, in close touching turns.

STEP 2

Now catch in a small bunch of the hackle fibers for the tail. They should be about the same length as the body and should lie on the top of the hook shank. Don't cut off the waste ends at this stage as this will make a step in the body. The waste ends will be tied down when we wind the thread forward.

STEP 3

Tie in the stripped Peacock quill at a point directly above the barb. Try to tie the quill in so that when you wrap it, the darker side of the quill will be at the back, nearer the hook bend. Now continue to wind the thread back towards the hook eye making an even base layer on which the quill will be wound. Stop about 2mm (1/8th") short of the hook eye.

STEP 4

The Peacock quill can now be wrapped forward in close touching turns. Again stop about 2mm (1/8th") short of the eye, tie off with two or three turns of the thread and cut off the waste quill.

STEP 5

Tie in the hackle by the stalk, presenting the "best" side to the shank, using two or three turns of thread.

STEP 6

Make two or three turns of the hackle and tie off using three turns of thread at most. The hackle should be swept back as shown, but not drawn under the shank.

STEP 7

The wing slips should be held in position between the thumb and forefinger and offered up to the hook shank for length, dull side to dull side/concave to concave. The wing should extend at least to the bend of the hook, but slightly longer will give a more elegant look. Once the length is established, take a turn of thread up over the wing between your fingers, passing down the other side, without any tension on the wing segment. This is called the pinch and loop method. The "pinch" between the thumb and forefingers should be loose enough so as to allow the thread to pass between. For a full explanation of this procedure see **Pinch & Loop** on page 25.

STEP 8

Now bring the thread up at the front, again between the two fingers. Tension can now be applied to the thread in an upward direction as shown in Figure 8. The whole idea of this procedure is to apply tension to the wing segments in a vertical direction, so that the feather fibers have no tendency to roll and split, but compress tidily one on top of another.

STEP 9

A quick look will tell you if the wing is set correctly. If it is, make a few turns, but no more than half a dozen, to secure it.

STEP 10

Trim off the waste ends of the wing butts as closely as possible and finish the head with neat turns of thread. Make secure by either whipping or take a couple of half-hitches. Complete the head with a careful coat of varnish.

Tinsel bodies, even when they are correctly tied can be a source of weakness in a fly. This is particularly the case when the tinsel being used is of the Lurex type. This modern type of tinsel has many advantages over the traditional metal, but strength is not one of its best features. You can make all tinsel bodies much more robust by the judicious use of varnish, during the tying procedure. A bit of patience is called for because you must let the varnish go tacky before winding over it - if you don't do this, it is easy to end up with a sticky mess. Note also that a thin layer of varnish is called for - if it forms drops on the hook shank, you have used too much. One last tip - don't be tempted to use your fingers. If you do, you will quickly transfer the varnish onto your tools and your other materials. You can use this technique to strengthen herl bodies as well!

Apply a layer of varnish over the thread underwindings, before winding the tinsel to the rear.

Apply the next coat of varnish over this tinsel. When it is tacky, wind the second layer of tinsel forwards and tie off at the head.

Goldhead Hare's Ear - *a fast sinking nymph*

Materials

Hook: Curved grub hook size 8 - 14

Thread: Brown 6/0

Bead: 2 or 3mm (5/64 - 1/8th") Brass bead

Tail: A bunch of hare's mask guard hairs

Rib: Fine gold wire

Body: Hare's fur, taken from the mask

The Gold Ribbed Hare's Ear (or GRHE as it is often called) is one of the classic all-purpose nymph patterns and has been around for many years. To our eyes the hare's fur may seem pretty nondescript but it seems to have a fatal fascination for trout of all species.

Because of its widespread success, the GRHE has spawned a whole family of variants. Almost all of these flies share the same body - hare's fur ribbed with gold wire - the other details may vary. Some have a separated thorax, with or without a wing case, others may sport some kind of winging.

One of the great success stories in modern fly fishing is the application of bead heads to standard patterns. The beads may be gold, silver or copper or even plastic or glass of various colors.

The features that make these patterns so effective can be summarized as follows. The bead provides weight which sinks the fly to a fishable depth very quickly (and keeps it there). The weight at the front provides an undulating movement in the water flow or when the fly is retrieved. The flash of the bead mimics the gas bubble which is a feature of the ascending pupae of many fly species.

The GRHE is an outstanding candidate for this treatment. A gold bead beautifully complements the body color and the gold sparkle of the ribbing. In practice the Goldhead GRHE fulfills all expectations, and is one of the most effective nymph patterns of modern times. It can be used in all conditions and at all times of the season. There are few patterns that are truly indispensable: the GRHE and its goldheaded variant are such patterns.

It should be noted that although the dressing normally calls for hare's fur taken from the ear, the fur may be taken from any part of the hare's mask (face). The important thing is to get a range of colors and include a lot of the longer guard hairs. If your fly looks neat when it is tied, it's wrong!

Goldhead Hare's Ear - *a fast sinking nymph*

Step-by-Step Tying Instructions

STEP 1

For this fly, some work is needed before we place the hook in the vise. Take the gold bead and slide it on to the hook from the hook point end, with the countersunk side towards the eye. Putting the bead on this way round will slighly mask the hook eye as it will sink slighly into the countersink. There will still be plenty of room to thread the hook and the countersink at the front gives added movement in the water.

Once the bead is on the hook you can set the hook in the vise, taking hold only of the bend of the hook. The bead is now glued into position. Slide the bead back out of the way and apply a drop of superglue to the hook shank behind the eye and then slide the bead forwards again into position.

From a position directly behind the bead, run the thread back to a point above the barb, in close touching turns.

STEP 2

Now tie in the tail fibers. Select a bunch of guard hairs from the hare's fur. The guard hairs are the longer stiffer, fibers. Tie them in to lie round the bend of the hook as shown. When this is done you should tie in a length of fine gold wire or oval tinsel to act as a rib.

STEP 3

Now form a loop in the thread about 10cm (4") long and then take the thread back up to the rear of the bead. A dubbing twister should then be set in the loop to hold it open. Lightly wax the thread on the inside of the loop (there should be no lumpy residue on the thread). Tease out the hare's fur and apply it along the inside of the loop - there should be plenty of the longer guard hairs in this mix. Try and spread the dubbing mixture out evenly.

STEP 4

Now comes the clever bit. Take hold of the dubbing twirler between thumb and forefinger and give it a spin. This spinning will trap the applied dubbing between the two strands of thread and produce a hairy "rope". A dubbing rope of this sort is ideal when you wish to produce a body with lots of "kick". The dubbed body should be slim but straggly, with plenty of longer hairs to give movement in the water. It is difficult to produce this effect by applying the fibers to a single strand of thread.

STEP 5

The next step is to wind the dubbing rope forwards in even turns. Before doing this, I find it easier to grip the end of the dubbing rope in the hackle pliers. Once this is done. the rope can no longer untwist and the twirler may be removed.

STEP 6

Take the dubbing forwards, ending up tight behind the gold bead (this will also help to hold the bead in place if the glue fails after some use). Pull the last turn tight in and then secure the end of the rope with two turns of the tying thread. Remember, we left it there when we first formed the dubbing rope. When the rope is tied down you can trim away any excess with a sharp pair of scissors.

STEP 7

Now wind the rib forward in even, open turns, pulling it quite tightly into the dubbed body. When you reach the rear of the gold bead, secure it with a couple of turns of thread and cut away the waste. The tying thread should then be made secure behind the gold bead with several whip finish turns or half-hitches. A drop of varnish will finish off the fly.

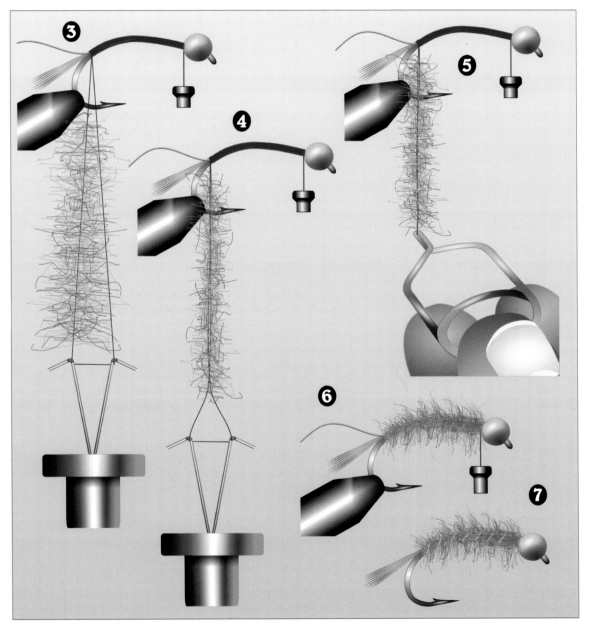

Achieving neatly varnished heads is often the bane of new tyers. So, for the beginner, here are a few tips which may help. Firstly let's consider the varnish.

Don't try to apply a varnish that has thickened up! If varnish has thickened (which it does) take a drop of the appropriate thinner, and thin it progressively, taking the mixture down to a liquid consistency only a little thicker than water. Apply this varnish and it will soak through the thread and will act more as a glue than as a glossy surface.

Forget all about brushes! Apply the varnish with as fine a needle as you can find. You will usually find that it takes anything from three to four individual drops on the tip of the needle to complete one coating on a size 10 hook. This thin varnish acts as a primer, thicker varnish can be applied subsequently over this.

When applying cement or lacquer to larger flies, build up the coatings slowly. Wait for each coat to dry before applying subsequent ones. If you don't wait, you'll achieve the 'prune' effect where a heavy build-up will wrinkle - almost impossible to fix.

For most varnishing jobs you should use a good quality cellulose such as Veniards' Cellire - it can also be thinned for use as a primer. An acrylic such as Firefly Liquid Glass or Hard-As-Nails nail varnish is ideal for a protective, hard finish.

The latter two are quite viscous, will hold a good 'body' and give a high gloss finish. With these high quality acrylics readily available we don't see much point in messing about with twin-pack epoxies, especially since the drying time can be murderously long. The acrylics will put on a coat almost as hard as epoxies, without any of the grief!

Don't apply black (or any other color) head cement directly over new head whippings. Even with the greatest of care, the black has the unhappy knack of leeching onto feather or hair fibre, transforming a neat finish into an untidy mess. Use the thinned clear varnish as the primer and follow this with the black in small, successive applications. Use black varnish only when absolutely necessary, clear varnish over black thread is better.

If, after making your 'perfect' fly, finished with a neat whipping, some light coloured fibers in the head have not been totally covered by the thread - don't despair! Use a fine black waterproof marker pen to blacken the rogue fibers, then apply clear varnish. This avoids the build up of unnecessary turns of thread.

Grey Wulff - *a Classic hairwing dry fly*

Materials

Hook: Down-eye medium weight dry-fly hook size 6 - 14

Thread: Red brown 6/0

Wing: Natural brown bucktail

Tail: Natural brown bucktail

Body: Grey muskrat or rabbit underfur

Hackle: Two blue dun cock hackles

This American fly from Lee Wulff is a classic fast water dry fly and is indispensable to fishermen throughout the world. On the English chalk streams the Gray Wulff is synonymous with the Mayfly but in fact it is representative of a great variety of duns and other insects. One of the classic patterns and arguably one of the top ten dry flies ever conceived.

Not surprisingly the original pattern Gray Wulff has spawned a whole range of variants, the best known of which are the Royal Wulff, the Grizzle Wulff and the Black Wulff. As a consequence of the success of the Wulff style of dressing, the use of hair as a winging material for dry flies has spread widely and in many cases has replaced the traditional upright split wings made of feather slips. The difficulty of tying traditional wings has much to do with the increased popularity of hair wings. The fish however do not seem to care greatly which method is used.

In our tying, the wing consists of a single bunch of hair. Purists will point out that a dry fly has two wings. The process of binding the roots of the wing together, as described in step 3 of the tying instructions can indeed be extended to divide the wing into two separate bunches, thus forming a classic split wing, but it is doubtful if this feature actually improves the fishing quality of the fly,

The hackle used for the Gray Wulff is a medium Blue Dun cock. For flies in the sizes 6 - 14 the best value that can be obtained is to invest in a genetic saddle from one of the top names such as Metz or Hoffman. A grade 2 or 3 saddle costs only a fraction of the price of a neck cape and will contain feathers up to 200mm (8") long. Just one of these feathers will tie many flies.

Grey Wulff - *a Classic hairwing dry fly*

Step-by-Step Tying Instructions

STEP 1
Set the hook in the vise and from a position about 3mm (1/8th") behind the eye, run the thread back to a point above the barb, in close touching turns.

STEP 2
Select a bunch of Bucktail for the wing and prepare it by first cleaning out any underfur from the butt ends. Once this has been done the hair should be placed tip downwards in a hair stacker and the tips evened up. This procedure is explained on page **Hair Wings**. Offer the Bucktail up to the hook with the tips pointing forwards, over the eye. Take four or five turns of thread to hold the hair in position and then check for length.

STEP 3
If the hair is the correct length. take some more turns to fasten it securely. Set the wing by lifting up the hair and taking several turns of thread, tight in front. This should cause the wing to sit almost upright, but with a forward lean. Take a few turns of thread around the base of the wing itself so that it holds together. When this is complete cut off the ends of the hair at an angle as shown. A few drops of varnish on the base of the wing at this stage will make it more secure. Return the thread to the rear of the hook, using just a few turns along the cut ends of the wing.

STEP 4
We can now tie in the tail. Prepare the hair in the same way as for the wing. Tie in the tail and check for length. When you are satisfied, take a couple of turns more to secure the tail. Now cut off the ends of the tail hair at an angle opposite to that used on the wing, so that the two dovetail neatly together as shown in the diagram.

STEP 5
Bring the tying thread forward in touching turns to the base of the wing and back again to the tail, forming a neat tapered base for the dubbing.

STEP 6
Load the dubbing by teasing out a small quantity of Muskrat or Rabbit underfur. Offer this material up to the thread and by twisting with the thumb and forefinger, in one direction only, form a spindle of material. Wind the dubbing forwards to the wing roots and secure with a couple of turns. Remove any excess material from the thread. The trick with dubbing is not to use too much material. Instructions on this procedure are given on page 19 **Dubbing**.

STEP 7
Take two Blue Dun cock hackles with a fiber length of about 1½ times the hook gape, which are matched for size. Trim away the flue at the bases and set them back to back. Tie these hackles in together at a position just behind the wing root, keeping the two hackles even. Grip the tips together in the hackle pliers and make two complete turns behind the wing and one turn in front of the wing.

STEP 8
Tie down the ends of the hackles with a couple of turns of thread and trim away the waste. A few turns of thread will make a neat head. Secure the thread with a whip finish or half hitches and finish off with a few drops of varnish. Be careful here! You do not want the varnish to run into the hackle so either use your fingers, or a hackle guard, to hold the hackle back out of the way whilst you apply the varnish.

In the Basic Flytying Techniques section of the book (page 20) we looked at a range of hackling techniques. The following tips may help you with various aspects of these techniques.

Tying in the hackle stalk

You may find that there is a tendency for the hackle stalk to pull out from its windings, particularly when you start to wind the hackle. Two things can help here. Firstly, use your finger and thumbnail (or the back of your scissors) to flatten the hackle stalk below the hackle fibers. Ensure that you flatten it in the plane of the fibers. The tying thread will grip better and the stalk will take up less room. Secondly use your finger and thumbnail to make a kink in the hackle stalk at the tying in position. This will make a groove which will locate the tying thread and again make things more secure.

Doubling a hackle

You may find that the hackle fibers simply don't want to fold back if you simply use your thumb and forefinger (see Collar Hackle on page 21). It can help if you prepare the hackle before it is tied in. Firstly, stroke the hackle fibers downwards, against the grain, until they sit at right angles to the spine. Now take the back edge of your scissors and run it along the top side of the hackle stalk towards the tip, gently but with sufficient pressure to "break" the spine. The hackle fibers will now fold backwards more easily.

Stripping a hackle

A full hackle may sometimes be too bushy for the fly you are tying. This may be the case when you are using a palmered hackle (see Palmered hackles on page 21) or when you are tying a "spider" type pattern, where a wispy, sparse head hackle is called for.

 In such cases you can strip the fibers from one side of the hackle stalk. To do this, grip the tip of the hackle in your left hand, making sure that you also have hold of the stalk. Now grip the fibers that need to be removed with the fingers of the right hand and strip them backwards, from the tip towards the butt end. If you do it correctly they will strip cleanly away from the spine, taking a small sliver of the spine material as well. The hackle can then be tied in and wound as usual.

This is also the correct way to select a bunch of hackle fibers for a tail or beard hackle - the sliver of spine helps keep the fibers together and they are much easier to handle.

TG Parachute Emerger - *a hatching fly*

Materials

Hook: Curved lightweight grub hook
size 10 - 16

Thread: Black 8/0

Wing: Calf body hair or Polypropylene yarn

Body: Cock pheasant tail fibers - natural
or dyed black or claret

Thorax: Hot orange seal's fur or sub

Hackle: Grizzle cock hackle

This is one of Terry's own patterns. It has been around for a few years but has not been widely publicized. The TG Parachute Emerger has proved equally effective for both brown and rainbow trout, especially on the large lakes and stillwaters.

The picture above shows the TG Emerger sitting in the surface film. The "angle of dangle" is critical to its success. This is set by the angle of the wing, so care must be taken to get this right.

The wing on this fly serves two important functions. Firstly, it acts as a post around which the parachute hackle is wound. Secondly, it acts as an indicator when fishing. The color of the wing is not actually critical but white shows up well against the water, enabling you to see where the fly is.

If you have difficulty managing the calf hair when tying the wing, you may find it easier to use Polypropylene yarn instead. This is easier to control and in fishing terms, makes little difference.

Flies tied with parachute hackling, float very well because the hackle fibers lie parallel to the surface film, rather than at right angles to it. Traditional hackled flies stand on tip toe and the sharp cock hackles tend to penetrate the surface quite easily in anything but very calm water.

The great advantage of parachute hackles for emerger flies, is that the fly body hangs in the water at a natural angle, exactly imitating the natural fly as it struggles to emerge through the surface film.

TG Parachute Emerger - *a hatching fly*

Step-by-Step Tying Instructions

STEP 1

From a position just behind the eye, run the thread back along the front part of the hook to make a secure bed for the wing. Bring the thread back to the center of the turns.

STEP 2

Now you can tie in the wing. Select a bunch of calf hair which is about 1.5mm (1/16th") diameter. Clean out all the unwanted fluff and underhair and tie it in with three or four turns of thread, at about the 3mm (1/8th") position so that it extends forwards about 1cm (3/8th") over the eye.

STEP 3

The angle of the wing is critical for this fly because it dictates the angle at which the body will hang in the water. Lift the entire wing between thumb and forefinger and take a few turns of thread, tight in front of the wing to push it upwards at an angle of 45 degrees. With the wing still held at the correct position, take a few turns of thread around the base of the wing to bind it into a slim post.

STEP 4

When this is completed, cut away the butt ends of the wing fibers at an angle as shown. Now run the thread backwards in neat turns to the bend of the hook, binding in the loose ends as you go. You need to produce a neat tapered body.

STEP 5

A drop of varnish on the wing root will help to secure the wing and provide a good base for the hackle later.

STEPS 6

At the end position, tie in a length of fine oval silver tinsel, followed by a bunch of pheasant tail fibers of the desired hue.

Bring the tying thread forward to the wing and then wind the pheasant tail forwards in neat turns. Tie off with two turns of thread. Now wind the ribbing forwards in even, open turns. At the base of the wing, secure with a couple of turns of thread and trim the waste of the ribbing and the pheasant tail.

STEP 7

Now you should tie in the grizzle hackle, pointing upwards next to the wing, as shown.

STEP 8

Take a small bunch of the thorax dubbing and wrap it sparsely around the thread. Take two turns behind the wing and one more in front, ending just in front of the wing. The thorax must not be bulky.

STEP 9

The parachute hackle can now be wound around the base of the wing. The first turn of the hackle will be the **top one**, all the rest will follow **below** this first turn. Take the tip of the hackle in the hackle pliers and make four turns in a clockwise direction, finishing with the tip pointing towards you. Now take the tying thread and twist it around the end of the hackle three or four times. Take the thread (with the intertwined hackle tip) twice around the bottom of the wing stump. With the hackle secure you can remove the hackle pliers and cut away the excess hackle. Instructions for this procedure are given in the **Hackling** section on page 20.

STEP 10

Take the tying thread forwards to the eye, beneath the hackle and secure with half hitches (a whip finish would trap the hackle fibers). Carefully varnish the head.

When tails or wings consisting of hair are used in a fly pattern, the hair taken from the skin may sometimes be straggly and misaligned. In this case it is often necessary to even up the tips of the hair so that they form a coherent group. There are some tyers who find that perfectly even tips give a slightly artificial "shaving brush" look to a fly. Actually, it depends on what kind of hair is being tied in, and for what purpose it is being used. The wing and tail of the Gray Wulff, illustrated on page 57, look much better if the hair tips are aligned. The same applies to the Elk Hair Caddis fly on page 43. On some hairwing lures there may be a case for a more unevenness, as the more tapered appearance of the fly may be more visually appealing.

There are many ways of evening up the tips of the hair, but the easiest and most consistent is by means of a hair stacker. Most hair stackers consist of two parts: an inner tube, and a base into which the tube fits. Using them is easy - the unordered hair is put tips down into the tube, the tube is put into the base and the whole assembly is tapped smartly on a hard surface. This sudden shock causes the tips of the hair to settle down evenly inside the base.

Do NOT do this on your dining room table!

Commercially available hair stackers are usually made of brass or wood. It doesn't actually matter what the material is, what is important is that the inner surfaces are absolutely smooth. Some cheaper models from third world countries are well finished outside, but rough within. The heavier the stacker, the greater the shock imparted to the hair, and the better it will settle down.

Cheaper alternatives can be made from old lipstick tubes or, for longer hair, plastic tubes of various kinds, previously occupied by tablets, sweets, cigars etc.

Duck's Dun - *a modern thorax style dry fly*

Materials

Hook: Down-eye lightweight dry fly hook size 12 - 18

Thread: Medium olive 8/0

Tail: Blue dun or bager cock hackle fibers

Body: Fine texture dubbing - bleached and dyed muskrat or synthetic

Wing: Two natural Cul-de-Canard plumes

Hackle: Blue dun cock hackle

The Duck's Dun is a modern dry fly dun imitation devised by Charles Jardine. There are two features of this fly that are of particular interest - firstly, it is tied in the "thorax" style - that is, the wing is tied in at the thorax position, some distance back from the hook eye. Secondly, the wing consists of two CDC plumes. CDC (Cul-de-Canard) feathers are fluffy filoplumes that come from around the preen gland of a duck. The preen gland supplies a copious flow of a natural oil which the duck uses to waterproof its feathers.

The plumes around the preen gland become saturated with this oil and are just about unsinkable.

In addition to their natural waterproofing, CDC plumes are well endowed with barbules which trap tiny bubbles of air, thus enhancing the floating qualities. Flies tied with CDC feathers are naturally buoyant and do not need treating with an artificial floatant. In the case of the Duck's Dun however, we do not want the body to sink under the water at all, so the body of the fly is normally treated with floatant.

The body color of a Duck's Dun can be varied, depending upon the natural fly that is being imitated. Most commonly used are shades of olive and brown.

The hackle on the Duck's Dun is normally clipped away beneath the hook shank quite short so that the fly sits flat in the surface film of the water just like the natural dun. The spiky effect created by the clipped hackle gives a "fussy" dimpled footprint in the water.

The Duck's Dun is one of the very best of the modern generation of dry flies and has very quickly become one of the standard dressings for stream fishing, both in the U.S.A. and in the United Kingdom.

Duck's Dun - *a modern thorax style dry fly*

Step-by-Step Tying Instructions

STEP 1

Set the hook in the vise, taking hold only of the bend of the hook. From a position about 2-3mm (1/8th") from the eye, run the thread back to a point above the barb, in close touching turns.

Before you tie in the tail fibers, you need to put a tiny ball of the dubbing material (about 1mm - 1/16th" diameter) on to the top of the hook at the tying in position for the tail. This little ball of dubbing is used to split the tail fibers into two groups in a forked configuration.

STEP 2

Now for the tail fibers themselves. Take the first bunch of two or three fibers and lay them onto the hook shank at the near side of the dubbing ball, using the ball as a shoulder so that the fibers splay outwards at an angle to the hook shank. When they are sitting correctly, take one or two turns of thread to secure them and then repeat the procedure for the fibers on the far side. Figure 2 shows the effect that you are trying to achieve.

STEP 3

Return the thread to the rear position and prepare a dubbing rope. Make sure that the dubbing is sparse and slim. Bring the dubbing fowards in even turns, making a slightly tapered body until you reach the tying in position for the wing. At this stage remove the excess dubbing from the thread.

STEP 4

Now tie in the prepared cock hackle. The length of the hackle fibers should be a bit longer than the hook gape at the widest point.

STEP 5

The next step is to tie in the wing. Select two natural CDC plumes - these feathers need to be about 15 - 19 mm (1/2 - 5/8th") long measured from the tying in position. Place the feathers tip to tip, convex side to convex side, so that there is a natural curve outwards. Place the feathers on edge, in position and take several turns around the butt ends to secure. Pull the first two of these turns in tight, so that the feathers are forced back against the shoulder of the dubbing. In this way the wing will cock up into position naturally at an angle of about 60 degrees. Trim away the butt ends and bring the thread back behind the wing.

STEP 6

At this point you should add some more dubbing to the thread and then wind one turn behind the wing, followed by two or three more turns in front, finishing just short of the eye.

STEP 7

Now take the tip of the hackle in the hackle pliers and after taking one turn behind the wing, wrap the hackle forwards through the thorax in even, open turns like a ribbing, keeping a steady tension as you do so. When you reach the front position, secure the hackle with two turns of thread and cut away the excess.

STEP 8

Finish the fly with several turns of thread, making a small neat head - do not overdo this. Make secure with a whip finish and complete the head with a drop or two of varnish.

Lastly, with your scissors, trim away the hackle lying underneath the hook shank.

Materials need to be stored in an orderly way if you wish to find the things you need, when you need them. There are very expensive, custom-made wooden storage cabinets available. These are beautiful but fortunately, not absolutely necessary. As a low-cost alternative, a series of cardboard archive boxes (used for storing documents and available from most office supplies shops) can be quite satisfactory. The individual feathers, furs and other materials can be kept in re-sealable plastic bags and simply placed in the appropriate box - one for hackles, one for furs, one for tinsels & threads etc. Card index drawers and other types of office storage systems can also be used and are often available second hand at low cost. Exactly how you divide and separate different materials is entirely up you you, so long as you are able to find things easily.

TWO WORDS OF WARNING

Parasitic Infestation
In the wild, most birds and wild animals carry natural infestations. These infestations can prove a serious problem once imported into the home environment. Feather mites can ravage and render useless a collection of fur and feather in a few days. It is strongly advised therefore that any plumage or fur which is brought in from the outside is dried and placed in a sealed bag, preferably with some Naphthalene crystals (moth balls). This can be checked from time to time, and at the first sign of any infestation, disposed of - hesitate at your cost! Fur acquired from "roadkills" should be skinned, washed and cured immediately, and stored as described.

Rabies
Those fortunate enough to live in countries free of rabies really never consider the horror of this virus. Caution should be exercised even if the temptation to pick up a roadkill is overwhelming. The rabies virus lives in saliva and nerve and brain tissue, and is usually transmitted by a bite. However, the virus can live on even after the death of the animal. It normally survives only a few hours in warm weather, but this period can run into days. If frozen, it can survive for two weeks and is able to become active again when the animal is thawed out.

For those determined to collect from roadkills, a pair of rubber gloves should be part of the kit at all times. Clorox kills the virus on contact, so drench the animal in this before setting about removing its skin. If it has gone into the freezer, it should be left un-touched for at least a month. Apart from the above general observations, tyers wanting to pick up roadkills in areas where rabies is endemic would be well advised to take advice from the local veterinary practitioner before even contemplating collecting materials.

Shrimp or Scud - *a sub-surface imitator*

Materials

Hook: Heaveyweight grub hook size 8 - 14

Thread: Olive 6/0

Weight: Flat lead strip

Shellback: A strip of polythene 2 - 3mm (1/8th") wide

Rib Fine gold wire

Body: Medium olive seal's fur or sub.

Hackle: Medium olive hackle fibers

The freshwater shrimp can be found in waters, both still and running, in all parts of the world. It forms one of the staple diet items for trout and grayling, especially in the early season. For this reason, having a good shrimp imitation to hand is always important. The pattern we have illustrated is a good close copy.

Colors can vary from pink and fawn, through greenish-grey to shades of olive. The colors used in this pattern can obviously be adjusted to reflect these variations.

In this dressing, Polythene is used as a shell back to represent the shiny shell of the natural. Other materials are often used, probably the most popular type being Spectraflash. This range of materials, usually available in sheet form, has an iridescent surface effect in various colors. it is ideally suited to imitations which will be used in colored or fast flowing water, the extra flash making the fly more visible to the trout.

There are many minor variations to shrimp patterns, some even have short tails, but most of them share the main features of this pattern: a dubbed, straggly hair body which imitates the legs of the shrimp, a stretched back which imitates the shell back of the natural and a ribbing which is used to represent the body segmentation present in the natural shrimp.

Other variations include the use of red or orange dubbing in the center of the body to imitate the red haemoglobin glow from within the shrimp's internal organs. The Traun Red Spot Shrimp is a very good example of this.

Apart from rainbow and brown trout, shrimp patterns are also deadly when fishing for grayling.

Shrimp or Scud - *a sub-surface imitator*

Step-by-Step Dressing Instructions

STEP 1
Set the hook in the vise, taking hold only of the bend of the hook. From a position about 2mm behind the eye, run the thread back to a point above the barb, in close touching turns and then back again to the starting position.

STEP 2
Lightly smear the hook shank with a drop of superglue and then offer the lead strip up to the top of the hook. Bind the lead down working back towards the bend. At the end of the thread, bend the lead strip forwards and bind it down back towards the head. Do this about 3 or 4 times, making each layer of lead shorter than the last to produce a humped shape.

STEP 3
When the lead application is finished, cover it completely with a layer of thread to even out any lumps and to produce an evenly tapered, humped body, leaving the thread at the rear position.

STEP 4
The next step is to tie in a length of gold wire for the ribbing. This is then followed by the polythene strip.

STEP 5
Now form a loop in the thread about 10cm (4") long and then take the thread up to the position behind the eye. A dubbing twister should then be set in the loop to hold it open. Lightly wax the thread on the inside of the loop (there should be no lumpy residue on the thread).

Tease out the seal's fur and apply it along the inside of the loop - in this case you can afford to be quite generous with the amount. Spread the dubbing mixture out evenly.

Now take hold of the dubbing twirler between thumb and forefinger and give it a spin. This spinning will trap the applied dubbing between the two strands of thread and produce a hairy "rope". The dubbed body of the shrimp should have plenty of straggly hairs to give life and movement.

STEP 6
The next step is to wind the dubbing rope forwards in even turns. Take the end of the dubbing rope in the hackle pliers. Once this is done, the rope can no longer untwist and the twirler may be removed. Take the dubbing forward in even turns until you reach the front position. Take a couple of turns with the tying thread to secure the rope and then cut away the excess.

STEP 7
Now take hold of the polythene and stretch it forwards over the back of the shrimp quite tightly. At the front position take several turns of thread over the polythene to secure it and cut away the excess. Wrap the ribbing forward in open turns, pulling it quite tightly into the back to divide it into segments. Work the wire backwards and forwards as you do this so that the minimum amount of dubbing is trapped. At the head, secure with the tying thread and remove the waste.

STEP 8
Select a bunch of cock hackles and tie them under the hook shank as a beard hackle. Take two or three turns of thread to secure the hackle and then trim away the excess stalks. Finally take some turns of thread to build up a small, neat head. The tying thread should then be made secure with several whip finish turns or half-hitches. A drop of varnish will finish off the fly.

Color Vision

One of the areas of flytying that causes a great deal of confusion among newcomers is the naming and description of colors. Generally, natural colors are not the solid, bright, pure colors possessed by dyes and paints. The natural color is usually more subdued and subtle. The most common names you will see are as follow:

Badger: This describes a feather with a dark central stripe and lighter tips. The center stripe can vary from dark red-brown through to black. The tips can vary from pure white through to an orange-yellow. The tip color is nominated by the qualifying name, e.g. a Golden Badger has tips of golden yellow and a center of dark brown to black.

Blue Dun: This is an almost indescribable color, from a brown-blue-grey tobacco smoke color which may stretch to a mousy grey-fawn. The tone of the color can vary from light, through to near black, the darker shades having a "steeliness" about them. The following list goes from light to dark: light blue dun, blue dun, dark blue dun, iron blue dun.

Coch-y-Bonddu: This is a variation of a badger coloration in which the colors vary from dark in the center, through light and back to dark again at the tips. The center and tips are a dark red-brown, the color between varies from ginger to a rich yellow.

Cree: This is a feather which is randomly marked with splashes of mixed colors. The splashes may vary from white, through ginger to a dark red-brown and black. The color of the feather is normally nominated by the most dominant color.

Greenwell: A special case of a badger coloration, so called because it is used to tie the famous "Greenwell's Glory" fly. A Greenwell feather has a central stripe which is very dark red- brown to black, with tips of a rich, orange yellow or ginger.

Grizzle: This term describes feathers that are colored with regular vee-shaped bands of black and white along their length. Grizzle hackles are also available with brown and white banding. Grizzle hackles are one of the most often used of all feather colors.

Olive: This is a green color with a tinge of khaki. It can vary from a light yellow through to a very dark green. The shade is described as light, medium or dark olive. Special cases are Golden Olive, which is normally a golden yellow, and Sooty Olive which is a very dark grey with a yellow-green tinge.

Red or Red Game: Natural red is not red at all, but rather a reddish, chestnut brown that may vary in tone from a light gingery color, through to a dark chocolate brown. If a bright, pure red is required in a dressing, it will normally be denoted as "dyed red". The tone is nominated by a qualifying word, e.g. light red, medium red, dark red etc.

Woolly bugger - *a sinking lure*

Materials

Hook: Long shank lure hook size 6 - 12

Thread: Black 6/0

Weight Fine lead wire 0.4mm (0.015") Diam.

Tail Olive marabou with a few strands of olive Krystalhair

Rib Fine gold wire

Body: Olive chenille

Hackle: Grizzle cock hackle dyed medium olive

The Woolly Bugger is a very successful American pattern that has proved its worth for rainbow trout in many countries. The form is not a specific nymph shape but rather a general outline that can suggest all kinds of food items to a fish.

Woolly Buggers can be tied in all sorts of color variations. The original tying was black but my favorite is the olive version which is shown here. Tied on a longshank 6 or 8 hook the fly makes a very good damsel fly nymph imitation, whilst smaller sizes may be taken for midge or sedge imitations.

Other color combinations that are worth trying are orange, and black with a green hackle and tail.

The Woolly Bugger may be tied with or without the weighted underbody but the weighted version has an undulating motion during the retrieve which the fish find most attractive. It can be fished on all types of lines but is ideally suited to use with an intermediate.

The Marabou tail has an aquatic mobility possessed by few other materials.

The combination of weight and marabou is a killing feature of many modern fly patterns.

The relative amounts of weighting and the length and thickness of the marabou are open to experimentation. One important point about marabou - if you find that the tail is too long after you have tied the fly, do not shorten it with scissors. The sharp cuts produced by doing this create a totally wrong impression. Should you need to shorten it, pinch off the excess between thumb and forefinger to leave the ends of the fibers tapered.

Woolly bugger - *a sinking lure*

Step-by-Step Tying Instructions

STEP 1

Set the hook in the vise, taking hold only of the bend of the hook. From a position about 2-3mm (1/8th") from the eye, run the thread back to a point above the barb, in close touching turns. If a weighted version of the fly is required, bring the thread back to the front position and tie in a length of 0.4mm (0.015") diameter, round lead wire. Wind the thread back to the rear position, followed by the lead wire in close turns. Tie off with a few turns of thread and remove the waste material.

STEP 2

Select a bunch of marabou fibers for the tail. As a guide, the bunch should be no more than 1.5mm (0,060") diameter when rolled together between the fingers. The marabou should extend backwards from the tying-in position by the length of the hook. If desired you can add a few strands of olive Krystal Hair to add a bit of sparkle. Tie down the tail with a few turns of thread and return the thread to the rear position.

STEP 3

Tie in a length of fine gold wire about 10 - 15cm (4 - 6") long, followed by a length of olive chenille. To prepare the chenille, strip away the outer coating for about 3mm (1/8th") to expose the core. Tie in using only the core and then bring the thread forward in close turns, tying in the butt ends of the marabou as you go. Stop at the front position.

STEP 4

Wind the chenille forwards in touching turns to the forward position, keeping an even tension as you wind. Secure the end with a couple of turns of thread and trim away the excess material.

STEP 5

Tie in the prepared cock hackle. This should be prepared and tied in as explained under **Palmered Hackling** on page 21. The length of the hackle fibers should be a bit longer than the hook gape at the widest point.

After the base of the stalk is securely tied in, take the tip of the hackle in the hackle pliers and after taking two complete turns at the tying-in position, wrap the hackle backwards in even, open turns, keeping a steady tension as you do so. When you reach the rear position, secure the hackle with two turns of the gold wire and cut away the excess. You will find that between five and seven turns of the hackle is about right.

STEP 7

Now take the gold wire between forefinger and thumb and wind it towards the head in evenly spaced turns, trying to keep the tension on the ribbing even as you do so. The gold wire should cross the hackle stalk in the opposite spiral, trapping down each turn as you wind forwards. You will need to wiggle the wire backwards and forwards as you do this so that you do not trap the hackle fibers. When you reach the front, secure the wire with a couple of turns of tying thread and then trim away the excess.

STEP 8

Finish the fly with several turns of thread, making a small neat head - do not overdo this. Make secure by a whip finish or a couple of half-hitches. Complete the head with a drop or two of varnish - do not use too much so that it runs into the hackle. Either use your fingers, or a hackle guard, to hold the hackle back out of the way whilst you apply the varnish.

75

INDEX

A

Anatomy of the Fly 2

B

Black Ghost 37
Black Pennell 29
Bobbin Holder 5

C

Chenille 12
Crystal Hair (Krystalhair) 12
Cul-de-Canard 11

D

Doubling Hackle 21
Dubbing
    Bodies 19
    Loop 20, 48
    Materials 9
    Needle 6
    Twirler 6
Duck's Dun 65

E

Elk Hair Caddis 45

F

Floss Bodies 17

G

Ginger Quill 49
Goldhead Hare's Ear 53
Gray Wulff .... 57\

H

Hackle
    Beard 22
    Collar 21
    Doubling 21
    Palmered 21
    Parachute 23
    Pliers 6
    Sources 11
    Throat 22
    Tying-in 64
Hair
    Bucktail 9
    Calf 9
    Deer 9
    Elk 9
    Squirrel 9
    Stacking 64

Hair Stacker 6
Half-Hitch Tool 6
Herl
    Bodies 18
    Sources 11
Hook Positions 40
Hooks 8, 40

M

Marabou 11
Materials
    List 12
    Storing 68
Montana Nymph 33

P

Parachute Emerger 61
Pheasant Tail Nymph 41
Pinch & Loop 25
Proportions when Tying 44

Q

Quill Bodies 18

R

Ribbing 19

S

Scud 69
Shrimp Fly 69
Stacking Hair 64
Styles of Tying 48

T

Tails 19
Thread 8
Tinsel 8
    Bodies 18
    Tying Tips 52

V

Varnishing Tips 56
Vise 5

W

Whip Finishing 14
Wings
    Feather Slips 24
    Hair 26
    Pinch & Loop 25
    Quills 11
Woolly Bugger 73